Jewish Dublin

PORTRAITS OF LIFE BY THE LIFFEY

AS RECALLED BY ASHER BENSON

JEWISHDUBLIN

Portraits of Life by the Liffey

AS RECALLED BY ASHER BENSON

© Text and compilation: The Estate of
Asher Benson 2007

British Library Cataloguing in Publication
Data

A CIP catalogue record for this book is
available from the British Library

ISBN-13: 978-1-906353-00-1

First published in 2007
by
A. & A. Farmar Ltd
78 Ranelagh Village, Dublin 6, Ireland
Tel +353-1-496 3625 Fax +353-1-497 0107
Email afarmar@iol.ie
Web www.aafarmar.ie

Picture editor: Edmund Ross

Typeset and designed by Bookworks

Index by Bookworks

Cover designed by Brosna Press

Cover photograph © Amelia Stein

Printed and bound by GraphyCems

Dedication

My purpose in dedicating this little book is to record my deep appreciation for the love of my wife, Ida, née Silverman, of Lithuanian–Romanian parentage, who was born in 1922 in Drogheda, Ireland and died in 2004 in Dublin; to my parents Millie, of Sosnowice, and David, of Czestochova, Poland; and to my sons Alan and Gerry, who with their families extend their ongoing devotion to me.

Then there were my dogs, Tinky, Rover and Ginger, all mongrels of the highest calibre; and my black cat, the Lady Clarissa, who guided me into old age.

This work—the subject matter confined to Dublin for reasons of space—has been produced by a committee of friends acting in an honorary capacity. The proceeds are donated to the Irish Jewish Museum in gratitude for the unfailing efforts of its curator Raphael Siev and a small band of volunteers, without which it would have long ago closed its doors.

Asher Benson
London Cockney, born 1921,
Dublin 'Blow-in' since 1946

Asher Benson

1921–2006

London East Ender and Second World War veteran (Indian and Burma) Asher Benson married Drogheda-born Ida Silverman in 1946 and they lived in Dublin until his death in 2006.

He was *Habonim* youth leader of groups in Brick Lane, Bow, Southport and Dublin. From 1979 to 1997 he was Ireland correspondent of the London *Jewish Chronicle* and Irish updater for the *Jewish Encyclopaedia*. He was a founder of the periodical *Dublin Jewish News* which appeared regularly from 1973 to 1987.

In 1978 Asher set up the Dublin exhibition *100 Years of Jewish Life in Ireland* and in 1984 he founded the Irish Jewish Museum in Walworth Road, Dublin.

A participant in the old 'Mabel's Table' group at Bewley's Oriental Café (see page 56), in his later days he completed the *Irish Times* crossword most mornings and played a mean game of bridge most evenings.

After the death of his wife Ida in 2004 Asher decided to record his personal knowledge and memories of the Dublin Jewish community, mainly in pictures, and although in his eighties and nearly blind, he achieved his ambition with a group of 'tireless friends', finishing the manuscript only weeks before his death.

Asher with his parents, East End of London, late 1920s

Asher's bar mitzvah photograph, Bishopsgate, London 1934

Asher (right) during the Second World War, 1940s

Wedding of Asher Benson and Ida Silverman in Greenville Hall Synagogue, Dublin, 1946

Asher on a Baltic cruise on the *Athena* in August 2006

Asher and Ida with their children Alan and Gerry *c.*1950

Contents

Patrons of *Jewish Dublin, Portraits of Life by the Liffey*

Edna and Max Abrahamson,
For Marie Berber and Beth Eppel

Joyce and Mossy Abrahamson,
For Leonard and Tillie Abrahamson

Taryn and Andrew Barling

Henry D. Barron,
For my dear wife Rosalind

Alan, Gerry and Leah Benson,
*For our parents and grandparents Ida and
Asher Benson*

Susan Benson,
For my dear father Sidney Glassburg

Jack Bloom,
*For my dear parents Alf and Hetty Bloom,
sister Doris Levy and brother Sydney Bloom*

Ian Bloomfield,
For Bella and Connie

Jack Bloomfield,
For Bella Bloomfield and Connie Hauser

Len Bloomfield,
*For life friends Bel Bloomfield and
Ida Benson*

The Borchardt Family

Sandra and Richard Brattman,
For the Bernstein and Rosenberg families

Sheila and Tony Brazil (Limerick),
For Anthony and Ellen Brazil of Meath Street

Carol and Ben Briscoe,
For Ida Briscoe and Rachel Isaacs

Joe Briscoe,
For Robert and Lilian Briscoe

Dr Stanley H. Buchalter,
For Cynthia Buchalter

Patricia Buchalter,
For my dear husband M. Don Buchalter

Moreen and Sam Caplin,
*For our parents Israel and Bertha Caplin and
Lew and Lily Gelberg*

Bertha and Maurice Cohen

Raynor Cohen and family,
*For Eric Maurice Cohen, Solly and
Esta Cohen and Percy 'Gussie' Freedman*

Alan and Carolyn Collins

Doris and Gershon Copperman,
*For Abraham Simcha Copperman and
Sara Zlate Copperman (née Saperstein)*

Billy Cornick,
For my dear wife Eunice

Louise and Quentin Crivon,
*For our dear parents Gertie and Sally Franks
and Sylvia and Sam Crivon*

Joyce and Selwyn Davies

Ian R. Davis

Suzi and Alec Diamond

Hilary and Tony Edwards

Michael Enoch,
For Mabel Enoch and Victor Enoch

Patricia Enoch,
For Rose and Joe Davis

Rose Esses,
For my dear husband Clem

Lily Fine,
For Eudice Fabian, Sheba Fishman

Derek Freedman,
On behalf of the Freedman family

Doreen Glassburg,
For my dear husband Sidney Glassburg

Carole and Graham (Gay) Golding
*For Esther and Dr Leslie David Golding
and Sybil and Harry S. Elliott*

Alan and Beverly Green

Hilary and Howard Gross

Marilyn and Ken Harris

Nick Harris,
For my dear wife Riv Harris

Pam and David Harris,
For our friend Gerald

Sybil Hazleton
For my dear husband Jessel

Danielle and Trevor Hess,
For Fanny and Nat Cristol

Lynn and David Jackson

Sonya and Martin Jackson,
*For Cecil Fine PC and
Herbert and Carmen Jackson*

Diana and Trevor Jacobs

Edythe and Howard Jacobs,
*For Sam and Henrietta Jacobs and
Ben and Lottie Robinson*

Dr Louis C. Jacobson,
For Mrs Marlene Jacobson

Hassia Jameson,
For Mrs Lesley Lewis

Marilyn and Alan Kron,
For Marilyn's dear father Leslie Watson

Lila Kronn and family,
For Dr Geoffrey Kronn

Carol and Peter Kutner,
For our dear beloved parents

Gertrude Lee,
For my dear husband Cecil Lee

Malcolm J. Lewis,
To mark the 60th Anniversary of the Dublin Jewish Progressive Congregation

Valerie Lowe,
For my dear husband Brian Lowe

Sandra Mamane

Brenda and Brian Mansfield,
For Kitty and Alf Mansfield

Irene and Gerry Mansfield
For Kitty and Alf Mansfield

Louis and Chookie Marcus

Estelle and Seton Menton

Thelma and Sol Moher

Dorothy and Stephen Molins,
For our beloved parents Seva and Alf Solomons and Molly and Al Molins

Sharon and Rodney Molins,
For Molly and Al Molins

Marionne Newman,
For my dear husband Victor Newman

Patricia and Cyril Newman

Paul Newman

Valerie and Richard Newmark

Sonia Patt, née Rosenthal,
For my dear parents Samuel Aaron Rosenthal and Rose Rosenthal

Chief Rabbi Dr Yaakov Pearlman and Rebbetzin Sheila Pearlman,
For Elizabeth Spain, a cherished friend

Cynthia Peller and Bernard Peller,
For our dear husband and father Gary Peller

Jennifer and Anthony Rosenshine

Edmund and Anne Ross,
For Edmund's parents Hannah and David Ross

Daphne and Ivan Selig,
For *Jessie* and *David Harrison*

Joyce and Alan Shaper

Carol and Alan Shatter

Denise and Alan Sherling

Ivor Shorts,
For Monty and Sabine Shorts

Asher and Rosel Siev
For Asher's dear parents Albert and Edith Siev

Rebecca and Martin Simmons

Thelma Simmons,
For my parents Samuel and Marjorie Noyek

Ingrid and John Simon

Audrey Sless, née Rosenthal,
For my dear parents Samuel Aaron Rosenthal and Rose Rosenthal

Mona Snipper,
For Maurice Snipper, a close bridge friend of Asher's

Jean and Henry Solomon

Richard and Rena Stein

Rosalind and Michael Stein,
For Sylvia and Abby Woolfson

Marilyn and Mervyn Taylor,
For our parents Abel and Miriam Taylor and Samuel and Millie Fisher

Queenie Watson,
For my dear husband Leslie Watson

Linda and John White,
For Linda's dear father Leslie Watson

Penny and Bernard White,
For Abe and Betty Esses and Hennie and Henry White

Dr Andrew and Valerie Woolfe,
For Valerie's dear father Leslie Watson and Andrew's dear parents Bessie and Hymie Woolfe

Dr Spencer N. and Gillian Woolfe

Acknowledgements

Ray Rivlin: *Shalom Ireland*, Gill & Macmillan, Dublin 2003. This comprehensive social history was the chief source of information on facts, people and places in the text.

Dermot Keogh: *Jews in 20th Century Ireland: Refugees, Anti-Semitism and the Holocaust*, Cork University Press, 1998

Nick Harris: *Dublin's Little Jerusalem*, A. & A. Farmar, 2004

Louis Hyman: *The Jews of Ireland, from the Earliest Times to the Year 1910*, Irish University Press, Israel Universities Press & the Jewish Historical Society of England, 1972

Bernard Shillman: *A Short History of the Jews in Ireland*, Eason, 1945

The Jewish Encyclopaedia: Funk & Wagnalls Company, New York & London, 1906

Carol Weinstock Silverander of California graciously gave permission for the use of a number of photographs taken between 1980 and 1985.

Amelia Stein, for photographs on pages 37, 60 (also on the cover) and 103.

Text contributions from Mossy Abrahamson, Gay Golding, Lynn Jackson, Cormac Ó Gráda, Manus O'Riordan, Colman Pearce and Ray Rivlin, and editorial assistance from Joan Finkel and Debbie Briscoe, are acknowledged with appreciation.

Our sincere thanks to our publishers Tony and Anna Farmar, and editor Warren Yeates for their helpful advice and encouragement in the production of this book.

Especially gratefully acknowledged is the help of members, friends and clergy of the Dublin Jewish community and of Raphael Siev, curator, and the volunteers of the Irish Jewish Museum. Without their advice, memories, photographs and written contributions this book could never have been put together.

Publishing board: Alan Benson, Gerry Benson, Michael Enoch, Edmund Ross, Marilyn Taylor

All contributions of pictures, and all work undertaken by Edmund Ross Studios and the rest of the publishing board have been donated voluntarily.

Every effort has been made to trace the copyright owners of materials, and to complete the book as Asher wished. We apologise for any errors or omissions.

Friends of Asher Benson working on the book: Edmund Ross (left), Michael Enoch and Marilyn Taylor (seated)

Introduction

'TAKI, ONLY SIX MONTHS OLD?'

THE END OF ANOTHER FOUR-POWER MEETING

'YOU NEEDN'T THINK YOU CAN GET AWAY WITH IT,' I TOLD HIM

Clanbrassil Street scenes (late 1940s) by photographer Oliver Samuel. These pictures appeared in *Nachlat Dublin* (*Dublin Region*, or *Dublin Heritage*), the annual publication of the JNF (Jewish National Fund), edited in the late 1940s by Asher Benson, and still appearing today.

It is just 350 years since the Lord Protector Oliver Cromwell tacitly permitted Jews to re-settle in Britain, from where they had been expelled in 1290. Those few Jews then in Ireland had of course been similarly exiled.

Around 1660 a tiny group of Iberian 'Conversos' (Jews apparently converted to Christianity in fear of their lives but secretly practising their ancient faith) sailed to Dublin and set up its first small congregation in Crane Lane. This narrow street then led from Dame Street down to the River Liffey, where the crane stood ready to load and unload the goods in which the Jewish traders dealt.

The location of the synagogue was pure conjecture until 1986, when Mr Stan Mason of Mason Technology bought Greenville Hall—a beautiful but sadly now redundant synagogue in the South Circular Road. With his keen sense of tradition he retained and incorporated many of the original features, an achievement of which he is justifiably proud. Touchingly, Mason Technology's address in Dolphin's Barn is still 'Greenville Hall'.

But the amazing coincidence which only then struck Stan Mason was that this was in fact the second time his company had come into possession of an Irish synagogue. They had previously acquired

premises in the aforementioned Crane Lane, a building with an unusual built-in gallery—where, in an Orthodox synagogue, the ladies sit. Unfortunately that building was later destroyed by fire.

In the 18th century the Jewish community continued to hug the Liffey, when its house of worship was relocated to a former glassworks in Marlborough Green, near the present-day Abbey Theatre.

The watery theme persisted with the St Mary's Abbey Synagogue known as 'Mary's Abbey' (formerly the first branch of the Royal Bank of Ireland), and seven minor congregations and two major synagogues—Adelaide Road and Greenville

Hall—dotted around the Portobello area near the Grand Canal. Terenure Synagogue, built in 1953, is not far from the River Dodder, and not too far away in Leicester Avenue is the Progressive Synagogue, founded in 1946.

In 1881 the Government Census return listed 394 Jews in Ireland. Following the viciously discriminatory May Laws passed in Tsarist Russia in 1882, numerous asylum-seekers reached Britain, Ireland and America, mainly fleeing from anti-Semitic regimes in Eastern Europe. Together with numbers of economic migrants, followed later by their families, the Jewish total peaked in 1946 at 3,907.

From 1900, for a further half-century, the heart of the community remained centred in the bustling South Circular Road and Clanbrassil Street area of Portobello, known as 'Little Jerusalem'.

Since then the Jewish population, which tended to move to south Dublin suburbs, has declined steeply, and now numbers under 2,000. Only one of these smaller synagogues of 'Little Jerusalem' survives, preserved as the Irish Jewish Museum in Walworth Road. It's worth noting that the 2006 Census, in its religious affiliation question, no longer includes 'Jewish' as a specified religion.

One purpose of this book is to illustrate how a tiny wave of immigration rolling on to the shores of Ireland, creating its own predominantly self-maintained religious, educational, charitable and social institutions, has made so substantial an impact on Irish life.

For example, in 1981, when the number of Jews in Ireland was 2,127, three Jews were elected to the Dáil (parliament), one from each of the main political parties, Fianna Fáil, Fine Gael, and Labour; and one of these elected members was later to become Ireland's first Minister for Equality and Law Reform. And in 1997 a Jewish judge was first appointed to Ireland's Supreme Court.

In this book we also hope, by illustrating the vibrant life of its Jewish community, to highlight this unique aspect of Dublin's social history.

So now, 120 years on from that earlier immigration, let us dwell on our current generation of newcomers, who, with larger numbers and enriching cultures, could benefit this country as this previous immigration has done; and as Irish and other emigrants have benefited the countries and cultures where they have settled, toiled and made good.

Asher Benson

Greenville Hall Synagogue, 1925

Clanbrassil Street

1930s–1980s

by RAY RIVLIN

Clanbrassil Street, on the south side of the River Liffey, was the hub of Jewish Dublin. Situated within the densely Jewish section of the South Circular Road and near the enclave known as Little Jerusalem, its kosher shops attracted the entire local Jewish community, as well as Jewish visitors from elsewhere in Ireland and abroad. Though fewer than one-quarter of its 90 private properties were occupied by Jews at any one time, the whole street appeared quintessentially Jewish. The kaleidoscope of movement and colour from both its fashionably attired and more traditionally garbed customers, their admixture of English and Yiddish, the pervasive aroma of *schmaltz* (salted) herrings and other *heimishe* (traditional) delicatessen, together with the pungency of yeasty bread and freshly killed meat and poultry, combined to make Clanbrassil Street more reminiscent of 19th-century Russia than of 20th-century Ireland.

Only rarely did anyone make a purchase and go straight home. Clanbrassil Street shopping meant calling on family and friends, meeting acquaintances, exchanging recipes and gossip, giving and receiving advice, even making a date or arranging a *shidduch* (marriage). It was a street where people lived and socialised. Children were born and reared there. It saw laughter and tears, hardship and prosperity, humour and pathos, rivalry and amazing solidarity in time of need.

Jewish shops in the Clanbrassil Street area *c*.1985 (from top):
Goldwater's poultry shop; Erlich's—Baila's butcher's shop, inherited from her father (page 78); Rubinstein's butcher's.

THREE MEN AND A HAT

'WOT! NO HADDOCKS?'

Clanbrassil Street scenes (late 1940s) by photographer Oliver Samuel. These pictures appeared in *Nachlat Dublin* (*Dublin Region*, or *Dublin Heritage*).

— 1 —

Clanbrassil Street was replete with characters such as Mrs Kronn who wore a Second World War gas mask when she grated horseradish; Berra Levi who plucked a Jewish child from a gypsy horse and cart with no idea as to whether he was being kidnapped or accepting a joyride; Harris Baigel the grocer, who had a barter arrangement with Mr Atkins the shoemaker, to exchange Baigel groceries for handmade Atkins' boots; and Myer Rubinstein, who shouted across the road to his son, 'Eileen had another girl. You're no bleddy good!' when his daughter-in-law produced a fourth daughter.

With no assets, no knowledge of running a business, and premises that were either small shops with living accommodation above or behind, or small dwellings with front rooms converted to shop use, the traders prospered through ingenuity, growing expertise and total indifference to the number of hours they worked. The 23 kosher shops trading in 1943 declined decade by decade as Dublin Jews moved away from the area or emigrated. Baila Erlich, the last of the traders, died in 1997, a fitting rearguard in the long line of hard-working, ingenious, generous and humorous, strangely naive

Cohen's antique shop, Liffey Street (1950s); the Cohens would only sell to those they liked.

traditional Jews who marked the passage of time in Clanbrassil Street.

Adapted from Shalom Ireland, a Social History of Jews in Modern Ireland *(Gill & Macmillan, 2003) by its author, Ray Rivlin. Ray, born in Dublin and reared in Belfast, is a history graduate with a Masters in Education. A retired secondary teacher, she has also written a number of educational textbooks.*

'Y'Irish', an Irish version of Yiddish!

FROM 1880S

The recently published list (The *Irish Times*, March 2006) of the 167 languages currently spoken in Ireland interestingly includes Hebrew and Yiddish, but sadly excludes 'Y'Irish'—a dialect of Yiddish and Irish much beloved in Dublin's Little Jerusalem.

Probably no more than thirty or forty words were involved, but in the 20th century they were used with such panache as to create the impression of a whole language.

The word *ferible* for example, dominated many agitated conversations among the Jews of the South Circular Road; it meant being *broiges* (a Yiddish as opposed to 'Y'irish' word)—that is, justifiably outraged. If you failed to be elected to a position on a committee which you were, in your own estimation, well qualified to hold, then you were *ferible* (or, you had a *ferible*).

And of course those quick to take offence were *feribledik* and had to be handled with kid gloves.

There was the celebrated case of one gentleman who, in furious resentment, stormed out of a meeting having, he felt, received a *ferible*. Inconveniently, the meeting was in his own residence!

The most long-lasting *feribles* were caused when relatives did not invite you to an engagement, wedding, bar mitzvah or even a circumcision celebration. Without doubt the record was held by Harold Mushatt, who, when asked why he was not present at a wedding, replied, 'I don't know. And as I'm related to both bride and groom I have a double *ferible*!'

Down in the Alley-O
Where we play Relievi-O
Up comes her mother-O
Have you seen my Mary-O?
Why did you let her go?
Because she bit my finger-O!
Which finger did she bite?
The little finger on the right.

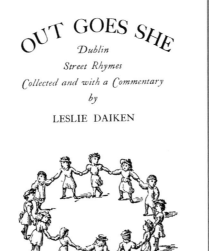

OUT GOES SHE
Dublin
Street Rhymes
Collected and with a Commentary
by
LESLIE DAIKEN

THE DOLMEN PRESS

Out Goes She, a book of Irish children's street rhymes published in 1964 by Dublin Jewish writer, journalist, poet and educationalist Leslie Daiken, of the well-known Yodaiken family. He had a great interest in children's toys and games, and his collection eventually became the basis of the National Toy Museum in Brighton. He also wrote widely and was involved in Irish literary life. His radio play based on Jewish life in Dublin *The Circular Road* was broadcast on Radio Éireann in 1959.

Daniel Mendoza, champion boxer

1760s–1790s

Pugilist Daniel Mendoza—'The Star of Israel'—of Spanish Marrano origin (Jews coerced into conversion to Christianity) was born in 1763. He was descended, according to Louis Hyman in *The Jews of Ireland*, from an impoverished Irish Jewish family of ten children, forced by circumstances to emigrate to England.

Mendoza was the first Jewish prize-fighter to become a champion. In 1789 he and a young brother came to Dublin where they gave boxing exhibitions at the newly opened Astley Theatre at the angle of Bride and Peter Streets.

Two years later in Dublin, Daniel was booked to fight 'Squire' Fitzgerald who, anticipating Muhammad Ali, tried 'stinging like a bee'. He was going to thrash the Jewish 'trickster' and stated that 'one Irishman is the equivalent of any number of Jews.'

At first Mendoza kept his cool, but as the anti-Semitic remarks intensified his temper frayed and amid tumultuous applause he well and truly clobbered the squire.

To give Fitzgerald his due, after the bout he said, 'If in the heat of the moment I used any expression that was insulting, I apologise to you.'

Mendoza was deeply touched by the warmth of his reception in Ireland and later recorded his appreciation of the friendliness shown by all he met.

Mendoza squares up, 1792

David Ricardo, first Jewish-born Member of Parliament for Ireland

1800s–1820s

It is generally believed that Bob Briscoe was the first Jewish member of a parliament (in his case the Dáil) representing Ireland. But this is only partially true: over 100 years earlier in 1819 David Ricardo, an English-born Jew, was elected to the British parliament as an independent representing the 'pocket' (sometimes termed 'rotten') borough of Portarlington in Ireland, which he served until his death in 1823.

Ricardo came from an Italian-Dutch Jewish family that had settled in England. Like his father he became a stockbroker at the London Stock Exchange. He committed the then heinous offence of marrying in a Protestant church; this, or possibly a financial dispute, estranged him from his family.

A brilliant economist, he was widely respected, and published his *Principles of Political Economy and Taxation* in 1817. From then until his premature death in 1823 this apostle of free trade remained a dominant figure in English economic circles.

Although there is no evidence that he converted to Christianity, he must have sworn allegiance to that faith in order to be admitted to Parliament. There he was an avid defender of religious freedom and rights for all beliefs, including that of Jews and Catholics in England and Ireland.

David Ricardo, Member of Westminster Parliament and distinguished economist, 1819

Mary's Abbey: the Dublin Hebrew Congregation and the 19th-century Laws & Regulations

1820s–1892

Myer Nerwich from Posen—then in Prussia—was the compiler of the Laws and Regulations of the Dublin Hebrew Congregation, published in London in 1839. This was three years after the purchase of the Seceders' Meeting House in Mary's Abbey, Dublin and its conversion into a synagogue. Every member had to buy a copy for five shillings; a fine was imposed if the tenets laid down were not obeyed.

The Dublin Jewish community had practically disappeared in the 1790s, but in 1822 was re-established in a small prayer hall on the upper floor of a congregant's house at 40 Stafford (now Wolfe Tone) Street. The accommodation was provided free by the owner, and so were the services of Nerwich, who was minister, cantor, secretary, treasurer and circumciser to the little community. No wonder he was often referred to as 'rabbi' and on one occasion in the *Dublin Directory* he was elevated to the rank of 'High Priest'. He continued to serve the new congregation in Mary's Abbey for some years. Mary's Abbey closed its doors one day before the opening of the first purpose-built synagogue of the Dublin Jewish community at Adelaide Road.

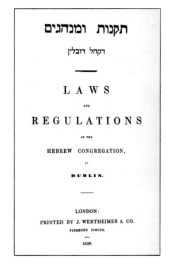

תקנות ומנהגים

דקהל דובלין

—

L A W S

AND

R E G U L A T I O N S

OF THE

HEBREW CONGREGATION,

IN

DUBLIN.

—

LONDON:
PRINTED BY J. WERTHEIMER & CO.
FINSBURY CIRCUS.

5599.

The top hat lying on its 19th-century container belonged to synagogue worthy Eli Schwartzman, who was the proud warden of the congregation.

Laws and Regulations 1839

Adelaide Road Synagogue, which served the Dublin orthodox community from 1892 to 1999. It was dubbed 'the English *shul* (synagogue)' by Eastern European immigrants because of the tendency to follow the style and customs of established British synagogues.

By trade, Nerwich was a jeweller and clock repairer, based in Crow Street. A gifted, devout Hebrew scholar, his comprehensive Laws mark him as a man of great intellect, especially as he was writing in a foreign language.

The original editions of Nerwich's publication are available in the National Library, the Gilbert Library, Pearse Street, and in the Irish Jewish Museum, Dublin.

The Zionist Movement in Ireland
1880S–PRESENT

Zionism (broadly speaking, the movement which advocated the Jewish people's return to Palestine and the re-establishment of their ancient State of Israel), had many adherents in Dublin, as in Europe, where its tenets fell on fertile ground. Where Jews lived impoverished lives, often persecuted, their spirits were bolstered for nearly two thousand years by the daily promise in their prayers that they would return to 'the land of milk and honey'—and above all to their holy city, Jerusalem.

This political climate at the end of the 19th century led many newly arrived Jews to enlist in *Chovevei Zion* (The Lovers of Zion), where for a few pounds small plots of ground could be bought in Palestine for new settlers. One or two of these genuine certificates of purchase are on view in the Irish Jewish Museum. Dr Theodor Herzl's World Zionist Organization encouraged Jewish support for the movement; in Dublin in 1902 the

Dublin Daughters of Zion, 1960

Bnei Akiva (religious youth group) Israel Independence Day Parade, 1951

WIZO group Hadassah's cake-making competition, 1970

Habonim (labour youth group) Israel Independence Day Parade, 1951

Jewish National Fund—still extant—was inaugurated, with its blue collecting box and slogan 'A penny a week is what we seek.'

The Dublin Daughters of Zion (DDZ) was founded in 1900 and those doughty ladies reigned supreme over Dublin WIZO (Women's International Zionist Organization) for nearly 80 years, at one time claiming a membership of 500–600. They raised funds through raffles and coffee mornings where they sold home-baked produce and 'nearly new' (sometimes rather old) clothing, furniture and anything else that fell into their net. With the other groups they participated in the WIZO annual celebrity concert in the Gaiety Theatre. All these successful fund-raising functions were largely organised by Dubliner Ethel Freedman—daughter of a Henry Street waxworks exhibitor.

DDZ, together with the other women's groups—Hulda, Hadassah, Hannah Senesh, South Dublin WIZO and Ziona—were affiliated to the Zionist Council of Ireland.

In its day Ziona was very active, uniquely mounting a cultural programme with regular speakers on a wide variety of subjects, debates, 'Follies' and evenings where the men were invited to make fools of themselves, and they shared an annual Dinner & Ball with the Jewish Medical Society in the Metropole or Clery's. It was rumoured that the Medical Society was a band of Ziona husbands whose wives were too busy with the Jerusalem Baby Home to bother with them.

There were also groups of religious men and women Zionists, and the Order of Ancient Maccabeans, a Friendly

Society. The long-established Friends of the Hebrew University and the United Jewish Appeal continue to fundraise, as they have done for 60 years.

At one time, in Rathdown Villas, Terenure there was a *Hachsharah* (preparatory training farm for agricultural work in Israel) in the form of a market garden. It catered for British and Dutch trainees and their neighbours were delighted to be able to avail of fresh cabbage at the house next door.

There were two strong Zionist youth movements in Dublin, each in its time accounting for over 100 youngsters, many of whom emigrated to Israel, often followed by parents. In *Bnei Akivah* the emphasis was on active religious Zionism. The middle-of-the-road *Habonim* (The Builders) had its own *bayit* (house) in Terenure. Later, numbers fell sharply, but after 40 years the name *Habonim* still appears in Hebrew on the right-hand pillar, now at the entrance of the *Machzikei Hadass* Synagogue.

Today there are only a few Zionist organisations, such as the JNF (Jewish National Fund) and the JIA (Joint Israel Appeal), and there is just one women's group—WIZO Ireland. But support and concern for Israel, the only Jewish State, and indeed the only democracy in the war-torn Middle East, is still strong among the Jews of Ireland.

In 2007 funds were raised for a gift of three ambulances to Magen David Adom, Israel's equivalent of the Red Cross, which serves all sick and wounded regardless of denomination, by the Jewish communities of Dublin, Belfast and Cork and their Christian friends.

Ethel Freedman, WIZO organiser, with her family

Irene Taylor (Guide Ranger) reading the Declaration of Independence at the commemoration of the foundation of the State of Israel, Maccabi 1958. Photo includes Cantor Gluck, Chief Rabbi Dr Jakobovits, John White, chairman JNF (Jewish National Fund) Youth Commission, Guide Commissioner Bertha Weingreen, and (background) Moishe Green, chairman Dublin JNF.

Michael Davitt and the Jews 1870s–1906

by MANUS O'RIORDAN

Michael Davitt was born in Straide, Co. Mayo in 1846. With the Great Famine of 'Black 47' the Davitt family emigrated to Lancashire. As a child labourer forced to earn his bread in a cotton-mill, the eleven-year-old Davitt had the horrific experience of having his right arm caught in factory machinery and amputated. Later he was a Fenian political prisoner in Dartmoor.

In 1879 he founded the Land League, which championed the rights of tenants and brought landlordism to an end in Ireland. In 1882 he was elected to Parliament on a Home Rule platform.

Michael Davitt has a special place in the affections of Ireland's Jewish community. In July 1893, in Ireland's leading newspaper the *Freeman's Journal,* he declared, 'The Jews have never to my knowledge done any injury to Ireland. Like our own race, they have endured a persecution the records of which will forever remain a reproach to the "Christian" nations of Europe. Ireland has no share in this black record. Our country has this proud distinction—freely acknowledged by Jewish writers—of never having resorted to this un-Christian and barbarous treatment of an unfortunate people.'

Davitt's opposition to anti-Semitic persecution and pogroms later reached a global audience. Francis Sheehy-Skeffington, his loyal disciple and biographer, wrote: 'In 1903 Davitt went to Russia

Michael Davitt 1846–1906, founder of the Land League

as special correspondent of the Hearst newspapers, to investigate the Kishinev Massacres, then exciting so much interest throughout the civilised world. He stayed only a short time in Kishinev, but long enough to make a thorough investigation into the facts. His conclusions, summarised in his letters to the *New York American,* appeared in more detail in his book *Within the Pale,* published after his return: "The tortures inflicted upon the Jews of Kishinev, with the connivance or active assistance of the authorities, gave him such a subject as eminently suited his impassioned pen."'

Unfortunately, in the following year that impassioned pen had also to address an outbreak of anti-Semitism in his own native land. As Sheehy-Skeffington related: 'For the Jews his sympathies never flagged. Early in 1904 a bigoted Limerick priest preached a sermon against the Jews, which became the starting point for a boycott directed against the members of that race in the city of Limerick and its vicinity. Starting on economic grounds, the attack soon developed features of racial and religious bigotry. It took little root, and speedily died away. Davitt was, however, the one public man to denounce it as an outrage upon the fair name of the Irish people, and to vindicate the Jews, as a race.'

Michael Davitt died on May 31, 1906 and was buried in his native Straide. Sheehy-Skeffington recorded one tribute of particular note: '…There was a wreath from the Jewish community of Dublin in grateful remembrance of Davitt's efforts on behalf of the one race which had suffered more than the Irish.'

(Francis Sheehy-Skeffington, Michael Davitt: Revolutionary Agitator and Labour Leader, *first published 1908)*

Manus O'Riordan is Head of Research at SIPTU (Services Industrial Professional & Technical Union) at Liberty Hall in Dublin. He has also carried out extensive research on anti-Semitism and other aspects of Irish Jewish history.

The 'Weekly' (*Wikla*)
1870s–1950s

On Israel Silverman's arrival from Romania, his first 'weekly', or *wikla* ('Y'Irish' for collecting weekly payments for drapery, see page 3) entailed him tramping the streets with a heavy black oilcloth-wrapped bundle on his back.

He graduated to a bicycle and then the luxury of a horse and cart, but according to Mr Coddington who held the reins, and unknown to Israel, the horse had previously belonged to the local fire brigade. When the alarm clanged, the animal would bolt in the direction of the fire, and wouldn't budge till it had been extinguished.

From humble beginnings 1860s–1870s
by CORMAC Ó GRÁDA

In mid-August 1868 a visitor from London named Ezekiel Margoliouth attended *Shabbat* (Sabbath) services at the Dublin synagogue, then located at Mary's Abbey, off Capel Street. Margoliouth was a Jewish convert to Christianity; his journal records his account of 'two glaziers from Russia', to whom Polish-born Margoliouth spoke in their native tongue. Thrilled at meeting a fellow Yiddish-speaker, the glaziers accompanied him through the city streets, as he declared to them that their Deliverer had already landed centuries ago. The glaziers' abject poverty made them sceptical of this claim, since they had been taught that once the Messiah arrived 'all Israel shall then sit every one under his vine and under his fig tree.'

I like to think of these two unnamed glaziers as the forerunners of a migration from Tsarist lands that would radically transform and enrich Irish Jewry over the next half-century or so.

The immigrants were not warmly welcomed by their Irish co-religionists. Nonetheless, it is only fair to state that as more indigent Litvaks arrived, the pre-existing Jewish community *did* help them. In 1878–80 about forty households received relief in kind. In 1878 one Jacob Davis of Chancery Lane received matzos, meal, sugar, and tea and coffee worth 17*s*. 5*d*. in all.

Chancery Lane, Dublin on the eve of the First World War

The Dublin Metropolitan Police, it seems, found accommodation for some of the earliest arrivals in Chancery Lane, about halfway between Dublin Castle and St Patrick's Cathedral. They lived 'in a little square wherein stood the police station, joining the other foreigners—Italian organ-grinders, bear-leaders, one-man-band operators, and makers of small, cheap plaster casts of the saints of the Catholic church'. Originally a small but elegant street of three- and four-storey buildings, by the 1870s two houses on the street featured on a list of tenements condemned as unfit for human habitation.

Some of the first immigrants to arrive can be named. The register of births records children born to Jacob Davis of 28 Chancery Lane (1874), Marks Isaacs of 78 Bride Street (1875), and L. Rosenberg of Moore Street (1875). A Jacob Davis of 14 Chancery Lane is listed as a painter in the marriage register of St Mary's Abbey on October 2, 1873, and his father is listed as a glazier. These details corroborate novelist Hannah Berman's remark that the pioneers moved first to 'streets and laneways not far from Jervis Street, Mercer Street, and Bride Street.' Indeed, the national school on Bride Street was the first to receive immigrant children. Molly Harmel Sayers, whose uncle Peisa would become for a time the richest man in the immigrant Jewish community, was born in a tenement house in Jervis Street: 'a delicate child, [she] survived only because of the tender care bestowed on her by a drunken apple woman.' She is presumably the Miriam Harmel whose birth was registered in February 1878; if so, her family moved to 20 Upper Mercer Street around this time. Jervis Street was not far from Moore Street where L. Rosenberg lived, or from St Mary's Abbey. Perhaps the presence, albeit temporary, of the Rosenbergs and Harmels in the Jervis Street area indicates the drawing power of a place of worship to these very observant Jews.

Soon the Litvaks would move south to the little maze of streets off Lower Clanbrassil Street, from which would spring Dublin's Little Jerusalem. In due course a Jacob Davis—one of our glaziers, perhaps?—would become *shammas* (beadle) of Oakfield Place *shul* (synagogue).

Ezekiel Margoliouth's journal is held in the library of the Representative Church Body, Dublin 14. I am grateful to Raymond Refaussé for alerting me to it.

Cormac Ó Gráda is Professor of Economics, University College Dublin. He is the author of several works on Irish economic history and, most recently, Jewish Ireland in the Age of Joyce: a Socioeconomic History *(Princeton University Press 2006).*

Miriam Copperman (later married to Abel Taylor) with her brother Abram Copperman c.1913. Abram and his wife Sadie were the parents of Gershon, Moshe, Yehuda (Yukie), Philip, Leila and Yitzchak, all now in Israel, where Yehuda established the unique Michlala seminary for young Jewish women in Jerusalem.

Ballybough Cemetery
1718–1908

The oldest Jewish institution surviving in Ireland is the ancient disused cemetery at 67 Fairview Strand. A small, well-preserved area, it is carefully tended by a remarkable husband and wife team and a little dog who live in the cottage fronting the burial ground, built in 1858. He is Con O'Neill, retired from the Irish Army, and she is Gloria, a former nun so devoted to her task that she has been seen hand-washing tombstones.

The cemetery was first leased in 1718 and the freehold bought 30 years later by the Bevis Marks Sephardi (Portuguese) Synagogue in London, which to this day retains the deeds. (Three hundred years ago the small Irish community was predominantly of Spanish and Portuguese origin.) The purchase price was £34. 10s.

The little graveyard encapsulates the history of the Irish Jewish community. It served the whole country, including Belfast, for 180 years until the end of the 19th century, when it went out of general use.

According to historian Louis Hyman, the earliest grave, almost unreadable, dates back to 1777. Notable is the tomb of Alderman Lewis Wormser Harris, who died in 1876, just after he had been elected but not yet appointed Lord Mayor of Dublin. If he had lived he would have been Dublin's first Jewish Lord Mayor. (Eighty years later, in 1956, Alderman Robert Briscoe became Dublin's first Jewish Lord Mayor.)

Ballybough Cemetery, dating from the 1700s. Clockwise from top left: tombstone of Ernest Wormser Harris, son of Lewis Wormser Harris, died 1946; tombstone of John Isaac Davis, died 5643 (1882); general view of the cemetery 2007; tomb of Alderman Lewis Wormser Harris, died 5636 (1876); caretaker's cottage, built 5618 (1858).

There were just three 20th-century interments—1908, 1946 and 1958—all members of the Wormser Harris family, which bequeathed funds for the upkeep of the cemetery arising from property they owned in South Great George's Street. Responsibility was vested with the Dublin Hebrew Congregation, but has now passed to the Jewish Board of Guardians.

Of course, there must be many more burials than there are tombstones; the latter were listed by historian Louis Hyman some 40 years ago as numbering 148. Many headstones were looted by residents of the area, and he recounts in his *The Jews of Ireland* (1972) the macabre tale concerning a Jew in 1816 visiting 'a Christian friend … and [perceiving] near the fireplace a stone with a Hebrew inscription … intimating that his father was buried in the chimney'!

According to Mrs O'Neill there is still considerable interest in the cemetery from individuals, tourists and cruise visitors, especially the three or four Rothschild graves, though there is no known connection with *the* Rothschilds.

Rather sadly she scans the surrounding area where the Celtic tiger is pawing up the dust, 'Look at the tombstones—the inscriptions are fading away…'

Dolphin's Barn Cemetery
1890S—PRESENT

Dolphin's Barn Cemetery beside the Grand Canal has been in use since the 1890s. Top photograph shows the cemetery's Prayer-House.

Estella Solomons, self-portrait 1908

Estella Solomons, artist
1882–1968

The portraits and landscapes of Estella Solomons, forgotten in Ireland for many years, have in recent times become admired and highly priced. Born in 1882 into an artistic and professional family, she first showed at the RHA (Royal Hibernian Academy) in 1905. She became involved in the national struggle, joined Cumann na mBan and assisted in the 1916 Rising, remaining active in the Republican cause all her life.

As well as the leading literary, artistic and political figures of the time, she also painted striking portraits of her family, prominent in the Jewish community: her father, Maurice, an optician with a literary bent and an abiding interest in Jewish education; her brother, Bethel, who was Master of the Rotunda (see page 23); and her mother Rosa, who was closely involved in the building of Adelaide Road Synagogue. Rosa was particularly interested in Jewish education for girls. Estella's portrait of her shows a dignified white-haired matriarch, who was in fact an inspirational figure in the community.

Estella's self-portrait shows an intelligent determined woman. She later married the poet Seamus O'Sullivan, but not till after the death of her parents, who would have been horrified by her marrying out of the faith. She died in 1968.

Portraits by Estella Solomons of her father, Maurice and mother Rosa, who headed a distinguished family living in Dublin for a continuous period of 180 years. Rosa did much social work in the community and was a poet of distinction.

The first little Jewish day school managed by Maurice Solomons in premises below the Adelaide Road Synagogue, 1900

The 'Jewish Union' 1908–1948
by MANUS O'RIORDAN

With a number of variations on its title of International Tailors, Pressers and Machinists Union, this trade union was established in 1908 by immigrant Jewish workers employed in Dublin's clothing industry. Although known colloquially in 'Dublinese' as 'the Jewish Union', the membership had a non-Jewish majority within its first decade.

The Jewish refugees who had fled Tsarist Russian pogroms to constitute the first set of leaders of this new Dublin Union were not yet literate in the English language. For that they relied on their first General Secretary, Henry Miller, an English-born Jewish tailor. In June 1909 they took their courage in their hands to engage in their first strike action. Within a month, through the mediation of a respected Jewish community leader, Philip Sayers, a settlement guaranteed representational rights. By 1912 the Union was also engaged in further industrial action against both Christian and Jewish

employers. To the Tailors and Pressers Union must go the honour of leading the struggle against sweated labour conditions in Dublin's clothing industry.

Isaac Baker, an immigrant Jewish peddler from Russia, employed by 1911 as a tailor, became a trustee of the Tailors and Pressers Union and in 1923 was a delegate to the Irish Trade Union Congress. He made a succinct but eloquent protest against anti-Semitism.

In 1948 the Jewish Union, finally known as the Irish Garment Workers Industrial Union, amalgamated with the National Union of Tailors and Garment Workers.

From 1912 to 1915 the head office of the Union was located at 52 Lower Camden Street, Dublin, which from 1892 to 1916 had also housed a synagogue.

In August 1914 a Union activist, Lithuanian-born tailor's presser Harry Levitas was married in that same synagogue to Latvian-born Leah Rick.

On 18 June 2002 their eldest son Max Levitas unveiled a commemorative plaque on the building in the presence of Ireland's Chief Rabbi Yaakov Pearlman, whose own grandfather was a Dublin tailor believed to have been a member of the same Union.

Max's younger brother Maurice Levitas (1917–2001) was a veteran of the International Brigade's Connolly Column that fought in the Spanish Anti-Fascist War, and he endured a year of imprisonment following his capture in 1938. This son of Dublin's 'Jewish Union'

was among that handful of surviving Connolly Column veterans honoured by the President of Ireland, Mary Robinson, on the occasion of her unveiling of the James Connolly Memorial at Liberty Hall in 1996.

Manus O'Riordan is Head of Research at SIPTU (Services Industrial Professional & Technical Union) at Liberty Hall in Dublin. He has also carried out extensive research on anti-Semitism and other aspects of Irish Jewish history.

Trade Union poster calling for public protest meeting, July 1913

Chief Rabbi Pearlman looks on as Max Levitas unveils a plaque marking the head office of the 'Jewish Union' in Camden Street, Dublin, June 2002. *Photo: Ruth Levitas*

Greenville Hall Synagogue

1925–1984

Greenville Hall Synagogue, the pride of Dublin's Lithuanian Jewish immigrants, was opened in 1925, and closed some 60 years later. Despite negotiations for it to become a mosque, it has ended up as a light machinery factory.

Ladies' Decorating Committee, 1925

The Ark of the Greenville Hall Synagogue, containing the *Torah* (the holy scrolls of the law)

Bride and groom signing the *Ketuba* (wedding contract) in Greenville Hall Synagogue, with the Reverend Gittleson

A wedding at Greenville Hall in the 1970s

Isaac Herzog, Chief Rabbi
1919–1936

Dr Isaac Herzog, a saintly and scholarly man, was appointed Chief Rabbi to the Irish Free State in 1919. An ardent religious Zionist, steeped in the Talmud (Jewish law), confidante and friend of statesman Éamon de Valera, his generosity was well-known.

He infused, as Bernard Shulman put it, a new religious zeal and made many improvements to the life and activities of the community.

His mastery of the Irish language within a short time of his arrival in Dublin earned him the sobriquet of 'the Sinn Féin Rabbi'. With Arthur Newman and others, he was responsible for the foundation of Zion Schools, the first and only Jewish National (primary) School.

He went on to become Chief Rabbi of then Palestine—after 1948 of course, Israel—but he always maintained contact with President de Valera and the Irish Jewish community. His son Chaim later became the only Irish-born President of Israel (page 31), and his grandson Isaac is now a Minister in the Israeli government.

Chief Rabbi Isaac Halevi Herzog
(1889–1959)

Arthur Newman
1920s–1960s

In the mid-20th century, the Irish Jewish community was fortunate to have a triumvirate of philanthropic businessmen who, it often seemed, put their charities before their livelihoods.

Maurice Ellis, together with Mick Jacobson finally got the Greenville Hall Synagogue opened in 1925—the First World War had put the building on hold—and later they funded the cost of Maccabi Sports Club's new pavilion. But this revelation is not typical of the two men, who, like the third member of the team, preferred to help people in trouble without any publicity.

Arthur Newman was a child when his father Louis brought the family to Cobh, where they disembarked apparently in the belief that they had arrived in America. After a period in Cork, the Newmans moved to Dublin where Arthur became a bespoke gents' tailor, making uniforms for British officers. At the end of the 1914–18 war, he manufactured demob (troops' demobilisation) clothing and then went into the retail clothing trade with his two sons, Ernest and Victor.

Arthur Newman will be particularly remembered for the conviction that the Dublin Jewish community needed a secular school that would also provide Hebrew religious instruction. With a determined man like Newman, thought gave way to action and with help from many others in the community the Zion National Schools, Bloomfield Avenue was born in 1934. The cost of the building was £12,000 and the government grant was £4,000. The Newman foundation stone can still be seen, though the building is now no longer a school. Newman's other communal work included the extension of the Adelaide Road Synagogue in 1925.

All three men found time to work on refugee committees and were staunch Zionists, arranging for charismatic Zionist leaders to visit and speak in Dublin.

Arthur Newman

Harold Mushatt, 'Kill or Kure'

1920s–1960s

Harold Mushatt exhibiting his wares in the Irish Jewish Museum 1985

Harold Mushatt was a man with a gifted memory. In the Adelaide Road Synagogue of which he was a worthy, he could stand before the donations board for the 1925 extension and give a potted biography of each of the 150 donors, and for good measure, his opinion of the size of their contributions.

He and his brothers owned the famous Mushatt's Pharmacy in the Dublin Liberties, which was in business from 1924 for 43 years. There they sold their own brand of remedies labelled *KK*. *KK Foot Paste*, for example, was for 'corns, welts, calluses and bunions—no need to use dangerous razors, knife blades or burning acids'.

It was claimed that *KK* stood for *Kill or Kure*, and although Mushatt's shop is long gone, *KK* medicines are still available.

Dr Bethel Solomons

1920s–1960

Gynaecologist Dr Bethel Solomons proved them all wrong when they said a Jew could never become Master of the Rotunda, a prestigious Dublin maternity hospital (the first in Europe)—a post he occupied from 1926 for seven years with great distinction.

This scion of Dublin's longest extant Jewish family had many other qualities. In 1946, with Larry Elyan and other like-minded individuals, Dr Solomons helped to found the Dublin Jewish Progressive Synagogue. A patron of the Irish arts, his keen visage surmounted by wide-brimmed hat could be seen patiently awaiting a new opening in the Abbey Theatre.

But his great pride was being selected to play rugby for Ireland: unable to contain his excitement he asked a stranger what he thought of the Irish XV. The reply was deflating, 'Fourteen Protestants and a Jew? You wouldn't call that Irish!'

Portrait of Bethel Solomons by his sister Estella Solomons c.1920

The Briscoe family

1920S–PRESENT

Outside these islands the public is rarely aware of the existence of Irish Jews, but one name that stays in many minds is Briscoe, particularly in the US where both Bob Briscoe and his son Ben were warmly welcomed for decades, especially around St Patrick's Day.

Father and son represented the Fianna Fáil (centre right) party in the Dáil (Parliament) for a continuous period of 75 years, from 1927 to 2002; in addition they served between them three stints as Lord Mayor of Dublin, in 1956 and 1961 (Bob), and 1988 (Ben).

Bob was the son of a pacifist Lithuanian immigrant to Ireland, who unusually named another offspring Wolfe Tone in honour of the leader of the 1798 rebellion against British rule. But above all, he admired the Irish constitutional leader Parnell.

In 1919, then aged 25, Bob was sent by rebel nationalist leader Michael Collins on a secret and dangerous mission to buy arms for the Irish War of Independence.

When Bob was elected to the Dáil, a lifelong friendship began with 'The Chief' (de Valera) which only ended when 'Dev', then President of Ireland, came to visit him in his last illness.

But despite this close friendship Bob must have been deeply saddened that during the Nazi regime in Germany and the Second World War, Ireland virtually closed its doors to Jewish refugees, including some of his own relatives.

Joe Briscoe congratulating his brother Ben on becoming Lord Mayor of Dublin, 1988

In the Jewish community Bob, acting as a 'bridge' to non-Jewish compatriots, was often called on to sort out problems. A lifelong supporter of the Zionist cause, he favoured Jabotinsky's Revisionist Party, whose leaders saw parallels in their own War of Independence from the British with the Irish struggle some 30 years earlier. When de Valera was invited to the young State of Israel in 1950, he asked Briscoe to accompany him.

Ben Briscoe is one of Bob and Lily Briscoe's seven-strong family of four sons and three daughters. A hard-working parliamentarian, who showed great care and concern for his constituents, he finally retired in 2002 after nearly 40 years in politics, having instituted the prized Lord Mayor's Awards for special achievements of citizens.

In the 1992 General Election, Ben was involved in a marathon re-count battle with Democratic Left for the final seat in Dublin South Central. After ten days of re-counting ballot papers, Briscoe was declared the victor.

Father and son had a long record of service to their constituents and faithfulness to their political cause, and the Briscoe name is synonymous in Ireland with the positive aspect of politics.

Of Lily and Bob's brood just one other remained in Dublin—Joe—who was involved both with the Jewish community and the Irish army.

Graduating from the wartime ARP (Air Raid Protection), he told a white lie about his age in order to 'bunk in' to the Local Defence Force: the year was 1945 and Private Briscoe just 15. He served until 1993 when there was a grand stand-down parade at Cathal Brugha Barracks in honour of Commandant Briscoe.

Joe also qualified as a dentist and on holiday in Manchester met Debbie; they married and settled in Dublin, both entering Jewish communal life with enthusiasm. Joe concerned himself with the public affairs committee of the Jewish Representative Council. This period, pre-dating as it did the appointment of a resident Israeli ambassador, was crucial in terms of the concerns of both the local Jewish community and of Irish relations with Israel.

Debbie still works with the Ireland–Israel Friendship League, the Council of Christians and Jews and other inter-faith bodies, and the Irish Jewish Museum.

Lord Mayor Bob Briscoe drops in to Zion Schools, 1957

Bob Briscoe with Rabbi Alony, first Jewish chaplain to the first Jewish Lord Mayor, 1956

Bob Briscoe with President John F. Kennedy on the latter's visit to Ireland, 1963

Joe Briscoe at his Irish Army stand-down parade in 1993 with his wife Debbie

The Tomkin family, medicine and music

1920S–PRESENT

(Left–right) Former Chief Rabbi Jakobovits, Dr Samie Levenson, Dr Harris Tomkin and Chief Rabbi Isaac Cohen at Stratford College 25th anniversary, 1977

Alex died in his 40s, leaving his charming Hungarian wife Julie and three young children, and unwittingly depriving hundreds of the gift of eyesight which was his to give had he lived longer.

Gerald, another son, has a hairstyle reminiscent of an absent-minded professor, but this diagnostic physician, specialising in diabetes, is a far cry from that first impression, because many patients are leading a normal life due to his skills. Moving with the Adelaide Hospital when it was relocated to Tallaght, Professor Tomkin recently concluded his tour of service there.

A third son, Dr David Tomkin, lectures in Law and Government at Dublin City University Business School. A solicitor, he has co-authored books and articles on corporation and medical law.

Dr Harris Tomkin was a man to remember because he practised for 60 years as an ophthalmologist in the Royal Victoria Eye and Ear Hospital in Adelaide Road, Dublin. In the middle years of the 20th century everybody in the Irish Jewish community seemed to go to Tomkin 'to get their eyes fixed'. He was interested in Jewish education and worked for Stratford College where he endowed a room in the new school.

He and his South African-born wife Suzy willingly hosted charity events in Clontra, their splendid Shankill estate, and welcomed members of *B'nei Akivah*, the religious Jewish youth movement, when they came a'camping on their doorstep.

Harris's son Alex followed in his father's footsteps as an eye specialist and quickly acquired a national and international reputation of the highest order. He was also an accomplished musician.

The Troubles
1920S

If you were in *schtoch* (difficulties) during the Troubles (1916–23) the man to consult was Michael Noyk, a Dublin-born Jewish solicitor who successfully defended many Sinn Féiners in the Irish War of Independence against Britain.

Military leader Michael Collins was a close friend and client, but more puzzling was Noyk's association with Sinn Féin leader Arthur Griffith who wrote: 'I have in former years often believed that the three evil influences of the century were the pirate, the Freemason and the Jew'. When they met, as they often did, Noyk could see no anti-Semite and Griffith could see no Jew, although Noyk was a life councillor and honorary solicitor of Adelaide Road Synagogue. When Noyk died in 1966, the Dublin Brigade of the IRA paraded at his graveside in Dolphin's Barn, according the military honour due to an old comrade.

Robert Briscoe also risked life and limb to run guns for the insurgents, but that tale is referred to elsewhere (see *The Briscoe family*, page 24).

When Leon Spiro bought a second-hand printing press, he hardly expected to be involved in Sinn Féin clandestine activity. But one of his compositors was Republican leader Oscar Traynor, and the IRA paper went out regularly from Spiro's Charlotte Street premises.

When the Troubles were brewing, the British government, with a beautiful sense of mistiming, appointed Sir Matthew Nathan as its Under Secretary for Ireland. Sir Matthew, a distinguished London-born military officer, had served in the British Colonial Office in Egypt and Sierra Leone, had been Governor of the Gold Coast (Ghana) and Hong Kong. The third chink in his armour was the fact that he was a Jew and he was, of course, subjected to three-prong attacks.

And then there is the mystery of the identity of Abraham Weeks or Wix, listed as 'A Jewish comrade who joined on Easter Monday (in the Revolt) and died in action'. Was Weeks a Dublin Jew? None can tell for certain.

Rev. Solly Bernstein, a lifetime of service
1930S–1990S

As Nick Harris observes in his book *Dublin's Little Jerusalem*, most long-term attenders at Terenure Synagogue (founded 1953) associate it primarily with Dublin-born Rev. Solly Bernstein, and his wife Bertha, affectionately known as Belke, who was born in Yashenovska, Poland.

A truly humble and pious man, he taught many bar mitzvah boys their portion of the Law in what was known as BBC (Bernstein's bar mitzvah class). He knew by heart the Hebrew names of all members of the community and their families, even after 15 or 20 years absence, and also if they were *cohanim* (hereditary members of the priestly caste) or *levites*; this information was required to call members to the Reading of the Law during Sabbath services.

Bertha, Solly's faithful and hard-working helpmeet, was famous for her cooking, especially her *milchike* (traditional yeast cake).

Together the Bernsteins gave a lifetime of service to the community and in particular to Terenure Synagogue. Their greatest pride lay in their three sons—Mashey, a writer and lecturer, Avraham (Om), a business executive, and their eldest son the late Isaac, a gifted rabbi, married to the late Ruth Gilbert.

Rev. Solly Bernstein at the opening of the Samuel Taca Hall, Terenure Synagogue, 1980s

Sam Noyek, timber merchant who, in the 1960s, with his brothers, brought Wareite (a plastic finish, forerunner to Formica) to Dublin interiors. He was a 'master-builder' of the Terenure Synagogue and worked tirelessly for it all his life.

Terenure Synagogue, built to seat 600 in 1953 and still in regular use. It is the last remaining major orthodox synagogue in the Republic of Ireland. Among its features are striking stained-glass windows on the north and south walls.

The Samuel Taca Hall beside Terenure Synagogue, endowed in the 1980s by Mrs Fanny Taca (centre) in memory of her husband

Engraved silver trowel used by Sam Noyek to turn the first sod of Terenure Synagogue

The Coleman sisters
1930s–2000

When their first novel *Full Circle* was published to acclaim, the two Dublin Jewish Coleman sisters 'couldn't believe how fast everything had happened.'

Sheelagh said, 'As a child I wrote non-stop. I had a couple of poems published. My ambition was to write short stories.'

Her sister Tessa recalls writing her autobiography at the age of 12, the doubtless lurid incidents of which were recorded 'downstairs at night on our old typewriter'.

The novel was at first intended as a tribute, revolving around their mother Dora. 'But,' remarked Tessa, 'the characters gradually took over', and *Full Circle* became the tale of an Irish family in the first half of the 20th century and the complications that arise when a Jewish boy and a Catholic girl fall in love.

Dora was born in 'Welsh Wales'—Swansea to be exact—and never lost her Celtic accent, even many years later when she appeared on stage with the Dublin Jewish Dramatic Society. In Manchester she married Bernard Coleman, a Russian Jewish immigrant. The couple moved to Dublin where their three children were born, 'the girls' and one son who emigrated to Israel.

Sheelagh married Dr Neville Boland, who held the first recognised clinics on allergies in Sir Patrick Dun's and Baggot Street hospitals, and was a genius with electrical gadgets. His proficiency at the piano is a musical trait that their sons

Sheelagh (right) and Tessa Coleman, 1995

inherited to establish themselves firmly on the Irish and international musical scene.

Tessa married an Israeli, Jack Cohen, who became a successful businessman, and they had two daughters and a son.

The Crivon family

1930S—PRESENT

Sam Crivon, a Londoner brought to Dublin at an early age, worked in a bank and studied at night. Eventually he became a well-respected Senior Counsel, who practised for over fifty years.

A man of even temper—which was just as well as he gave legal advice to committees in the Jewish community, some at loggerheads with each other—he became a Life President of Adelaide Road Synagogue.

Sam's pipe-smoking son, Quentin, is a solicitor and partner in O'Hagan Ward, of which earlier partners were Norman (Nissie) Gruson and former Government Minister Richie Ryan.

Quentin became chairman of the Association of Combined Residents' Associations (ACRA), campaigning for the abolition of domestic rates.

He served as Chairman of the Jewish Representative Council, during which period President Herzog of Israel made his historic visit to the land of his birth.

Quentin's Belfast-born wife Louise, a barrister, served on the Legal Aid Board and has been involved with communal and synagogue affairs.

Sam's brother Robert (Ruby) Crivon taught classics at Trinity College Dublin. During the Second World War, as Lieutenant-Colonel in Intelligence, he was involved with the Japanese surrender negotiations in 1945.

He later became Assistant General Secretary in the Council of Europe and briefly joined the United Nations in Paris.

Quentin Crivon

Kennedy & Carr

1930S & 1940S

Kennedy & Carr were a successful musical partnership of which Jimmy Kennedy was the better known member. Jimmy, born in Omagh, Co. Tyrone, was responsible for numerous classic popular hits, including *Red Sails in the Sunset* (written in Portstewart), *The Isle of Capri, Teddy Bears' Picnic (1932), Harbour Lights* and *South of the Border (Down Mexico Way)* (with Michael Carr).

Kennedy, a modest man, contrasted sharply with Michael Carr, who was boisterous, liked the best of clothes and food and was very fond of the ladies.

According to Noel Cregan, proprietor of the Copenhagen Café in Rathmines, Michael Carr was a Jew, the son of 'Cockney' Cohen, who owned a café in Hawkins Street beside the long gone Theatre Royal. The enormously successful *Did Your Mother Come From Ireland?* originated in a conversation Michael overheard in a Dublin train.

When Kennedy enlisted in the British Army, Carr was said to have followed him around as he was on patrol one night. Object—the final draft of *We're going to hang out the washing on the Siegfried Line, have you any dirty washing mother dear?*

Chaim Herzog, former President of Israel

1930s–1980s

President and Mrs Herzog (1st & 3rd left) with President and Dr Hillery at a State dinner in 1985

President Herzog on his state visit to Ireland in 1985 with his wife Ora (right) meeting his former teacher

Chaim Herzog is the supreme example of the local boy who made good. Born in Belfast in 1918, he was still a baby when his father was appointed first Chief Rabbi of Ireland. His childhood was spent at 33 Bloomfield Avenue and he attended Wesley College, a Dublin Methodist secondary school, before completing his education abroad.

He became a lawyer, but this was only one of the hats he wore; he followed careers in journalism, broadcasting, the Israeli army, military intelligence, politics and diplomacy, and capped them all by being appointed President of Israel in 1983.

In 1985 he was invited to Ireland on a State visit, and one of his tasks was the opening of the Irish Jewish Museum, ironically situated in a small former synagogue dubbed 'The Rebel Shul' because its members had opposed the appointment of Chaim's late father, Isaac Herzog, as Chief Rabbi (see page 22).

He also visited his old school, Wesley College, and later had an emotional meeting with his former teacher, an elderly lady who travelled especially to Dublin to greet him. Listening to him on the radio, members of the community who had known him were delighted to discover that he had not lost his Irish accent.

The Collins family and Zion Schools

1930s–1980

In 1934 Bill Collins, ex-British Navy, and his wife Cecilia were appointed caretakers to the newly founded Zion Schools in Bloomfield Avenue, the first Jewish National School. At the time their son Christy was one of the only two Christian pupils. They were much loved and respected, and the shock and sadness were palpable when, two weeks after the Second World War began in 1939, Bill Collins was lost with 518 others when their ship, *HMS Courageous*, was torpedoed by a German U-boat off the south-west coast of Ireland.

After that, as author Ray Rivlin puts it, 'The Collins family became part of Zion School life.' When Christy—whose Hebrew was good enough for him to stand in for a pupil in the Purim Festival play—died after years of caring service to the school, 'Zion pupils lined the street as a mark of respect.' Cecilia looked after generations of pupils as lovingly as any mother, as did her much loved daughter Maura.

Maura continued to help out even after her retirement in 1980, and was invited to many Jewish functions. Although her health declined, she is still, with the help of long-time principal Tom Hanley, in touch with the school she loves.

Information from Shalom Ireland *by Ray Rivlin.*

Mrs Cecilia Collins, 'second mother' to hundreds of Zion Schools pupils

Zion Schools

FOUNDED 1934

Zion Schools in Bloomfield Avenue was the first purpose-built Dublin Jewish school in which both Hebrew and secular education were combined.

It served the community for some fifty years, after which, as Stratford National School, it moved to Stratford College, Rathgar, providing, with the kindergarten, three levels of Jewish education. The primary school, with its interesting mix of children from different backgrounds, is now presided over by dynamic principal Tom Hanley.

Teachers and pupils in the 1960s, with headmaster Mr Cassidy

Zion Schools, 1960s

Teachers and pupils, 1960

Stratford College, Zion Road, Rathgar, now a well-regarded Dublin secondary school. Although a Jewish school, it has numerous pupils from diverse backgrounds. Long-serving principal Mrs Colette O'Broin (1978–99), and the current principal, Ms Patricia Gordon have helped to build its fine reputation. The façade of the elegant Victorian building has been well maintained.

A. J. 'Con' Leventhal

1920s–1960s

In 2006 Dublin theatre celebrated the centenary of Samuel Beckett's birth. Although the playwright's great buddy A. J. Leventhal was born ten years earlier, the similarity of certain aspects of their careers is striking.

After Leventhal graduated brilliantly from Trinity College Dublin in 1925, he took over Beckett's appointment as lecturer in French; Beckett, followed by Leventhal, went on to live in France, where both men ended their days.

A. J.—writing as L. K. Emery—played a crucial role in helping to establish Beckett, who never forgot the debt he owed to the academic.

Leventhal, known as 'Con' or 'Conti', is said to have acquired his nickname from the brass plate outside the office of his father's small trading business, which bore the grandiose inscription 'Continental Agent.'

Con's father Yudel and his mother Rose were a brilliant pair. Rose was a strong Zionist, and for 44 years held honorary office in the Dublin Daughters of Zion (DDZ), one of the many women's Zionist groups. This diminutive gentlewoman, who wrote poems and songs of Zion, successfully controlled committees of vociferous ladies who wore impressive hats for all occasions, and the organisation raised considerable funds for the welfare of women and children in what was then Palestine.

Portrait of A. J. Leventhal by Estella Solomons

When Rose retired in 1948 there were about 500–600 subscribers to the DDZ—astonishing in a community numbering less than 4,000 souls.

Con was reared in Oakfield Place in Little Jerusalem and he described tensions between 'Oakfield Israelites' and the rival Christian boys' gang of 'Lombard Westerners'. It appears that not too many heads were cracked.

James Joyce's work captured his imagination and in 1921 he visited the author; there was a discussion of the Jewish names that were to appear in *Ulysses*. Joyce, apparently highly appreciative of his contribution, was said to have rewarded him by singing *Hatikvah*, the song of hope that later became Israel's national anthem. As with Beckett, Con's critical assessment played an important

role. When *Ulysses* was described by a critic as 'pornographic' it brought the appropriate rejoinder from Con: 'One might as well call the Venus de Milo indecent.'

Throughout his life Con was a keen supporter of the Jewish national cause, and from 1948, of the newly established state of Israel, and recalling his mother Rose, there can be little doubt as to the origin of his interest.

He also had a strong attachment to the Irish Jewish community.

When Con died, Beckett, in a rare public display of feeling, set up a Trinity College postgraduate travelling scholarship in the name of his old friend. Many prominent authors contributed to the sale in aid of funds for the project; Beckett himself gave a manuscript and signed copies of limited editions of his work.

Bernard Shillman and his mother, Ada Shillman
1930s–1960s

Bernard 'Barney' Shillman was a mid-20th-century Jewish Senior Counsel who specialised in employers' liability, workman's compensation and licensing law. A stalwart of the Jewish community, he is perhaps best remembered for his *Short History of the Jews in Ireland*, published in 1945.

Bernard Shillman, from a charcoal sketch, 1934

But Bernard's great love was Zion Schools (opened in 1934), a groundbreaking institution open to all denominations, of which he became Hon. Secretary.

His mother Ada Shillman, originally from Cork, had been for forty years from her arrival in Dublin in 1892, a skilled midwife. Among the thousands of Irish men and women she helped into the world, two were mentioned in her son's book: Robert Briscoe, the first Jew elected to Dáil Eireann (Parliament), and Arthur Shields, later famous as an Abbey actor and Hollywood film star.

Ada was also involved socially and communally, and helped found St Ultan's Infant Hospital in Charlemont Street, and the Dublin Jewish Ladies' Charitable Society for the relief of expectant mothers.

'Tariff Jews'
1930s

When Seán Lemass was appointed Minister for Industry and Commerce in 1932 he was instrumental in helping the 'Tariff Jews' to come to Ireland. Bolstered with protection against imports from abroad, a number of Jewish manufacturers set up businesses—mantles, shoes, furniture and tailoring.

Sam Brown, who arrived via Liverpool, lived at 4 Walworth Road (which later was added to Walworth Road Synagogue at No. 3 and eventually became the Irish Jewish Museum). In his showroom in Mary Street he displayed good quality ladies' garments that he trade-named *Pioneer*, presumably with teetotal customers in mind.

Solomon Verby was also a manufacturer of ladies' clothing with a showroom in Dame Street. His efforts helped to inspire the foundation of the Jewish Home in the 1950s, and he campaigned enthusiastically for office on the Jewish Home committee, his slogan being particularly memorable: 'Don't be nervy, vote for Verby'.

A large London gents' tailoring firm, Polikoff of Mare Street, Hackney, London established themselves in Kilmainham, and the Spiro brothers set up a factory in Little Longford Street where they manufactured 'ladies costumes and mantles'. Later they were involved in Imco, the dry cleaning business.

IN MEMORY OF
SOLOMON VERBY
שלום דוד ורבי ז״ל
A FOUNDER OF
THE JEWISH HOME OF IRELAND

Solomon Verby, businessman

The Weingreens, two Lieutenant-Colonels

1930s–1990s

Jack and Bertha Weingreen in uniform, 1946

At first glance Jack and Bertha Weingreen seemed an unlikely pair: Manchester-born Jack was a short, gentle pipe-smoking man with no shirt-size small enough to fit his neck; in contrast his South African wife Bertha was never slow to forcibly express a point.

Appearances are deceptive—Jack was in fact an intellectual colossus who strode across the 20th-century international academic scene. A brilliant student, he was appointed Professor of Hebrew at Trinity College Dublin in 1937, and two years later published his *Practical Grammar for Classical Hebrew*, which, 70 years on, is still in extensive worldwide use.

The content, logic, depth and refreshing simplicity of style of his lectures captivated his audience, both academic and lay. Many of Ireland's Church leaders were his pupils, one of whom once described him as 'the finest Christian in Ireland.'

As a young man he became interested in archaeology, and participated in digs with the legendary Professor Yadin in (then) Palestine—later Israel. Reputedly it was in that country that he met Bertha at a bus stop.

In 1977 Trinity College opened the Weingreen Museum of Biblical Antiquities in honour of the Professor, using artefacts from his expeditions.

Bertha, a woman of strong character, was, like Jack, a convinced Zionist and founded several WIZO (Women's International Zionist Organization) groups in Dublin and Belfast. For some years she ran an elocution school. She was also a Division Commissioner of the Irish Girl Guides, which included the Jewish Brownies, Guides and Rangers.

The photo depicts the couple in the uniform of British Army lieutenant-colonels, an honorary rank accorded to them as members of the Jewish Relief Unit in which they were serving when the concentration camp of Bergen-Belsen was liberated in April 1945. Both agreed this was the most heart-rending yet morally rewarding time of their lives, and they were grateful to be able to help Holocaust survivors in some way.

An amusing sidelight of their military rank occurred just after the war when they were touring the BAOR area (the British-controlled part of Germany). Wiring in advance for accommodation they requested a room with double bed for 'two lieutenant-colonels', much to the consternation of British Army authorities.

The Weingreens' tale is a great love story: Bertha tended Jack like the child she never had, and looked after all matters of routine. Together they entertained friends from all walks of life to delightful teas in their conservatory, amid Jack's prized collection of cactuses.

On the day Jack died she seemed to succumb with him, referring to him as though he was still by her side. 'Tomorrow', she would say poignantly, 'Jack and I are invited to the Bishop's palace.'

Jack and Bertha Weingreen in 1993 *Photograph © Amelia Stein*

The Ellimans, kings of Irish entertainment
1910–1970s

Old 'Dubs' passing through Hawkins Street find it difficult to suppress a sigh of nostalgia for the Theatre Royal—the 4,000-seater pinnacle of the Elliman ventures in the world of Dublin entertainment. A couple of shillings bought three to four hours of solid entertainment, consisting of films and a live show featuring turns like Noel Purcell, his diminutive friend Mickser Reid and a chance to win £1 or £2 on a Double Your Money Quiz.

Maurice, an impoverished Russian-Jewish immigrant arrived here in 1894 aged 16. Unable to understand the Immigration Officer's request, he pointed to an advertisement for Elliman's Embrocation and was allocated the name by which the family has since been known. He lodged with the Smullens, whose 16-year-old daughter Leah he married, and with whom he had a brood of nine sons and three daughters, most of whom entered the family business.

A chance gift from his friend Joshua Samuels of a magic lantern—early moving pictures in which Joshua himself saw no future—set Maurice on the cinema trail and in 1911, in a disused garage in Pearse Street, he opened shop for the first time. Later came the De Luxe in Camden Street which, as its name hinted, was the last word in cinemas with '400 upholstered seats'.

During the Easter Rising in 1916 the Metropole Hotel was destroyed. From its ashes rose the jewel in the Ellimans' crown—a cinema with ballroom above available for weddings, bar mitzvahs and balls where Dublin's young couples, Jewish and otherwise, danced the night away. In the later years downstairs there was the stylish Metropole Grill, where unlimited hors d'oeuvres from the trolley cost a half-crown. A toupéed Mícheál Mac Liammóir dissected his plate of smoked salmon as he listened appreciatively to the deep tones of Irish *chanteuse*, Peggy Dell.

The Queen's (where Noel Purcell began his career) and the Savoy at one time or another entered the Elliman orbit, as did the old Corinthian, which wags called 'The Ranch' because of the number of 'cowboy pitchers' in its programme.

The Ellimans bought the Gaiety Theatre in 1936, and full control of the Theatre Royal followed shortly. Irish talent was nurtured under the Ellimans. Dick Forbes, Jimmy O'Dea, Cecil Sheridan and Maureen Potter made regular appearances from the 1940s. But the Ellimans also attracted international stars of stage and screen, including Judy Garland, Betty Hutton, Bob Hope, Danny Kaye, the Three Stooges, Gracie Fields, Dirk Bogarde, John Mills, Stewart Granger, Nat King Cole and James Cagney.

When the Abbey Theatre was destroyed by fire in 1942, Louis, Maurice's son, offered the Queen's in Pearse Street as a temporary home. And film-making in Ireland was greatly enhanced when he helped to found Ardmore Studios.

The extent of Elliman's philanthropy will never be known as Louis did not choose to publicise his acts of generosity, but many people in the profession as well as the Jewish community were quietly assisted, as was the Walworth Road Synagogue, the family place of worship.

When Louis Elliman died in 1965 aged 62, actress and comedienne Maureen Potter suggested the Gaiety should be renamed 'The Louis Elliman Theatre'. It would have been a fine tribute to this doyen of the world of Irish entertainment.

Louis Elliman receiving President and Mrs de Valera at a gala performance in 1960

Sam Lynn (left) on stage with famous actor Mícheál Mac Liammóir

'The Abe'—Professor Leonard Abrahamson 1920s–1961

by MOSSY ABRAHAMSON

Leonard Abrahamson was born in Russia and brought as a child to Newry, Co. Down. In his youth he was an outstanding scholar. A doctor full of kindness, compassion and good humour, he specialised in cardiac problems as Professor of Medicine at the Royal College of Surgeons. But in fact he practised all parts of medicine in a manner which endeared him to his patients; they could consult him about anything.

A most witty after-dinner speaker, he once told the story of a patient who was eternally grateful to him whilst in the nursing home but objected to his bill on the grounds that he only called to see him briefly in the morning and evening. He replied that his patient must remember that he worried about him all the time.

Socially popular, he owned racehorses (one was named Burnt Offering, to the amusement of his Jewish friends in the famous social and card club in Harrington Street, of which he was president). His involvement in Jewish life, which emerged in particular from the friendship and counselling of Chief Rabbi Dr Isaac Herzog, resulted in his becoming President of the JNF (Jewish National Fund) and of the Jewish Representative Council of Ireland. He was, as writer Ray Rivlin puts it, a natural leader of the community.

She adds, 'After his death the Jewish community paid tribute to him by endowing a Leonard Abrahamson Memorial Lecture at the Royal College of Surgeons in Ireland and planting trees in his name in Israel.'

Of Leonard's children, Maurice (Mossy), a former stockbroker, barrister and director of Allied Irish Bank played an important role in the Public Affairs Committee of the Jewish Representative Council of Ireland. The late Mervyn (Muff), Professor of Pharmacology at the Royal College of Surgeons in Ireland, emigrated to Israel in 1973 with his wife Marcia; he was appointed head of internal medicine at the Rebecca Sieff Hospital in Safed. The late Beth, married to Dr Ellard Eppel, was actively involved in Dublin WIZO (Women's International Zionist Organization). Of Leonard's twin sons Max is a consultant solicitor specialising in Engineering Contract Law, and David was awarded an MBE in 2002 for services to psychiatry in Britain.

Professor Leonard Abrahamson (third from left) beside his wife Tillie (née Nurock), presenting an ambulance on behalf of the Jewish community for use during the Emergency in the 1940s

David Beerman ploughing at Millisle Farm

Helga Dresna feeding hens: 'The aim was to become as self-supporting as feasible.'

Millisle Farm, a haven for Jewish child refugees

1938–1946

The beautiful but remote Ards Peninsula in Northern Ireland seems an unlikely place to have a Jewish connection. But at a previously derelict farm in the village of Millisle, Co. Down, a group of Austrian, German and Czech Jewish child refugees found a haven. They had escaped Nazi persecution through the Kindertransports—a scheme organised by volunteers of various religions whereby 10,000 Jewish children were brought to safety in Britain just before the Second World War.

With the help of older Zionist pioneers, adult refugees, and with aid from the Belfast and Dublin Jewish communities, a Northern Ireland Joint Council of Churches and the British Refugee movement, a self-supporting co-operative farm was set up and successfully run on kibbutz lines. Young people who travelled from Dublin in the summers to help on the farm never forgot the experience, and many befriended the refugees, at least 300 of whom passed through the farm in the war years.

The true story of how these young refugees, uprooted, racked by homesickness and fear for their families left behind, managed to make a good and productive new life in Northern Ireland and later, further afield, is told in *Faraway Home* (O'Brien Press 1999), an award-winning book for young people by Dublin author Marilyn Taylor.

After the war, a group of child concentration camp survivors were brought to Millisle Farm, and some still remember the healing effect of that peaceful and beautiful place.

The farm closed and passed into private hands in 1948.

Walter Tauber in the fields at Millisle

Rescue from Belsen— Suzi and Terry, Zoltan and Edith

1945–1948

When British troops liberated the Bergen-Belsen concentration camp in April 1945, near the end of the Second World War, they found more than 50,000 people barely alive under appalling conditions. The stench of death could be smelt from 15 miles away.

A group of doctors from Ireland, including Bob Collis, a paediatrician at Dublin's Rotunda Hospital, joined the British Red Cross and St John's Ambulance to help set up a small hospital at the camp, in an attempt to save some of the children, many orphans, dying daily from typhus, TB and malnutrition. Also helping was a Dutch nurse, Han Hogerzeil, who together with her mother, had courageously helped to run a safe house for Jews during the war.

At Belsen they cared for a group of orphan children, including six-year-old Terry and his little sister Suzi—originally Tibor and Zsuzsi Molnar from Debreczen, Hungary—and Zoltan and Edith Zinn. Suzi and Terry's mother had died shortly after liberation, and Zoltan and Edith were also orphans. In his book *To Be a Pilgrim* Bob Collis describes how six-year-old Terry insisted on sleeping with his little sister, weakened by typhus, protectively held in the crook of his arm.

After a period of recovery in Sweden, Bob Collis and Han brought their 'special

Jewish refugee children arriving in Dublin, 1946

Suzi and Terry with other refugee children

A recent photograph of former refugees Suzi Diamond and Zoltan Zinn-Collis

children' to Ireland, where they stayed first at Fairy Hill, an open-air hospital on the hill of Howth. Bob Collis and his wife adopted Zoltan and Edith Zinn; Terry and Suzi were adopted by a Jewish couple, Willie and Elsie Samuels.

Though never forgetting the tragedy and violence from which they had been rescued, they grew up in peaceful Ireland, married here, and had children. Their miraculous survival—1½ million Jewish children were killed in the Holocaust—can be seen as giving the lie to Hitler and the Nazis and their planned 'final solution', the total destruction of the Jewish people.

Bob Collis and Han later married, and became the first Irish people to be honoured with the title *Righteous among the Nations* by Yad Vashem, the Holocaust Authority in Israel.

Sadly, Terry Samuels died in 2007. But before that he had spoken to groups, on radio and TV about his horrific experiences. Today Suzi Diamond and Zoltan Zinn-Collis, together with the only other Irish Belsen survivor Tommie Reichental, and also Geoffrey Phillips, a former Kindertransport refugee, frequently visit schools and youth groups in Ireland speaking of their experiences—a living reminder of the ever-present danger of racism, intolerance and anti-Semitism on which the Nazi evil was based.

Zoltan's story is told in his memoir, *Final Witness: My Journey from the Holocaust to Ireland*, by Zoltan Zinn-Collis with Alicia McAuley (Maverick Press, 2006).

The Emergency

LATE 1930S–1945

In Ireland, the Emergency began in 1939, when the Second World War was imminent. But for European Jews it started in 1933 when Hitler and the Nazis were voted into power in Germany, and lasted until 1945 when the Nazis were vanquished after their evil policy of a fascist Europe and the extermination of all Jews narrowly failed in its objective.

The Dublin government, like so many others, closed its doors and the Department of Justice put heavy locks on them, shutting out the pitiful cries for help from those in dire danger of their lives. Any stray German Jews who managed to infiltrate illegally to Dublin were to be referred to the German Embassy to see if they could arrange for them to be repatriated to Germany!

The few refugees who arrived here before September 3rd 1939 were mainly people with family connections or who had the wherewithal to set up factories, of which the Irish Republic was in urgent need. What was a successful Jewish Viennese dentist to do when he escaped to Dublin? Obviously he starts a zip-fastener factory, which is what Hans Lowy did with the aid of an Irish partner. Similarly a ribbon factory was set up by Emil Hirsch in Longford, *Les Modes Modernes* by Marcus Witztum in Galway, and a hat factory in Castlebar, Co. Mayo.

Some tried to help the overwhelming numbers seeking to flee Europe's concentration camps—the Jewish Refugee Committee, the Co-ordinating Committee for the Relief of Christian Refugees from Central Europe, and somewhere between, the remarkable writer Hubert Butler, author of *The Children of Drancy* who, working for the Society of Friends, successfully saved many refugees who had assembled in the Kagran suburb of Vienna.

Many Dublin Jews also enlisted in the Irish auxiliary forces, the LDF (Local Defence Force) and the LSF (Local Security Force).

In 1946 when London Rabbi Dr Solomon Schonfeld had persuaded the British Chief Rabbi's Religious Emergency Council to acquire Clonyn Castle in Delvin, Westmeath for 100 young Jewish orphan concentration camp survivors from Europe, the tall, handsome army chaplain thought it would be plain sailing; but he had not reckoned with the Irish Minister for Justice, Gerald Boland, who stood firm against the project until lobbied in person by former Chief Rabbi Isaac Herzog. Even then the children were only allowed to stay for up to a year. Just to reinforce the welcome, shortly before

Welcoming Isaac Herzog, Chief Rabbi of then Palestine, is Ireland's Chief Rabbi Jakobovits and a delegation, including Irish Rabbi Theodore 'Teddy' Lewis (tall figure to the right). Rabbi Herzog had travelled to Dublin to lobby on the issue of Clonyn Castle.

Gay Golding, ready to hunt with the Ward Union Staghounds, Ashbourne, Co. Meath, 1959

Colman Pearce in action in 1976

Reminiscences of Little Jerusalem 1940s–1950s

by COLMAN PEARCE

My parents, born in 1913 and 1914 respectively, were both raised in that area off the South Circular Road affectionately known as Little Jerusalem.

One of my mother's best friends as a youngster was Bloomie Rubenstein, who later married Albert Sharpe; they and their children Melvyn, Geoffrey and Myra lived across the street from my family in Emorville Avenue. My mother Lily, and Bloomie (later a kosher caterer) continued to be good friends up to my mother's death in 1960.

My sisters Setna and Orla were very friendly with Myra Sharpe, who sometimes accompanied our family on beach trips to Donabate. My father Charles often mentioned that he grew up with Jewish youngsters, but many had moved away during the 1920s and 1930s. Among them he recalled Chaim Herzog, later to be a well thought of President of Israel.

Apart from the Sharpes I can remember other Jewish households on Emorville Avenue: Sid Davis and his wife in No. 19; the three Menkin ladies (Mama and

daughters Irene and Betty), and the man of the house Joe Menkin—they lodged with the Barnes family at No. 24. Other families on our road included the Lees, Eppels, Sievs and Kahans.

Nearby Carlisle Street also had Jewish families, but I'll never forget Mr Rubenstein from 24 Ovoca Road. One of our childish (and mischievous!) games was hitting door knockers and running. I was only caught on one occasion, when the long-suffering Mr R—obviously lying in wait for the next annoying 'phantom knock'—sprang like a greyhound from his house, caught me after a few feet and gave me a well-deserved clip on the ear. In sheer fright, I almost wet my pants!

My mother often said, 'the best Christians among our neighbours are Jews'! This was meant as a sincere compliment, as she found so much kindness and empathy with our Jewish neighbours. I was regularly asked by the orthodox Jewish families, as were my peers, to perform minor tasks on the Sabbath—turning lights or gas on or off etc. We delighted to do this, as the rewards were always interesting (money!) or tasty (sweets, homemade fudge or—our favourite—Matzo crackers). We always considered ourselves fortunate to perform these little tasks in homes that were basically the same as our own, but also, mysteriously, magically and intriguingly different—and a little exotic.

My family and I were blessed to live in a community that was not the typical homogeneous society in the Ireland of those times. We learned to tolerate and enjoy the differences that ethnicity and religion can offer. It was a prophetic look into the future of what is now a multifarious society in modern Ireland. Shalom!

In a long and distinguished musical career, Dublin-born Colman Pearce was principal conductor of the RTÉ Symphony Orchestra from 1981 to 1983 and has since been principal guest conductor with other prestigious orchestras. A successful composer and pianist, among his numerous recordings is The Memory is a Living Thing, *a CD including some of his own music.*

Miriam Taylor (née Copperman) with her children Gertie (Lee) and Mervyn at the beach *c.*1936

Touring Dublin Zoo, 1953. Gerry and Alan Benson, now Dublin businessmen, are third and fourth on the right (front row).

Bewley's: Mabel's Table—Wolfe and Leo Cherrick

1950s–1960s

It was the custom for a number of Jewish businessmen to sit together at lunch in Bewley's Oriental Café in Grafton Street. Their usual table was in the all-male smoking room beside the toilets in the basement. When this hideaway was later invaded by indignant females they moved up a floor to sit near the Johnston's Court entrance.

Collectively they were known as 'Mabel's Table' because the waitress of that name ruled over them, kept intruders away, and expected a postcard from holiday destinations addressed to 'Mabel's Table, Bewley's, Grafton Street, Dublin'.

The occupants included the brothers Wolfe and Leo Cherrick. Wolfe, an antique dealer, whose initials W. C. were the same as the famous British wartime Prime Minister Winston Churchill, wore a black Homburg hat. He claimed he often sold off his own hats as Churchillian relics to gullible tourists.

Leo had been a not very successful bookie but he still loved a flutter. He had a gap in his upper teeth where he lodged the cigarette he was smoking. One evening he was participating in a game of poker, debating his next move. 'Your turn Cherrick,' said his foe.

The cigarette quivered as he rejoined, '*Mr* Cherrick to you.'

'That's a lovely name for a horse I've just bought. May I call it Mr Cherrick?'

'Of course,' said Leo, and within a week the horse was dead.

'The story of my life,' Leo would sigh.

Leo and Wolfe Cherrick—not twins, but they could be.

The Marcus and Lentin families

1940s–PRESENT

The extended Marcus–Lentin family, 'blow-ins' to Dublin (i.e. born nowhere near the River Liffey!), hails from Cork, Limerick and South Africa, leaving aside the countries from which their parents and grandparents originated. Yet their impact on Irish cultural life has been most dramatic.

In Cork, Louis Marcus played the violin in the city's Symphony Orchestra, but the entrancing flicker of rolling film drew him to his life's ambition and this, combined with his love of the Irish language, put him behind the camera producing documentaries for Gael Linn in Dublin. He worked successfully for Irish and British television companies and was appointed to the Arts Council.

Chookie, his South African-born wife, was for many years—until her retirement in 2006—head of Stratford College Kindergarten. Intended primarily for Jewish infants, it now serves toddlers from many backgrounds.

Louis' big brother David Marcus, a lawyer, doffed his wig for literature. After a spell in London, he returned to Dublin to edit 'New Irish Writing' for the *Irish Press* newspaper, establishing the reputations of numerous Irish writers. In that context he met Ita Daly, a young novelist who would become his wife.

When attending the launch of a book by Maeve Binchy, David said, 'If Maeve can do it, so can I!' The result was the successful *A Land Not Theirs* portraying the Cork Jewish community in the Irish War of Independence.

Louis Lentin is a Marcus cousin born in Limerick, who in 1961 moved to Dublin. In the new Irish television service he progressed from floor manager to the Drama Department, of which he became head in 1979.

When Israel was invaded in the 1967 Six Day War he volunteered to help the tiny country battling for its existence, and in this land of miracles, was invited to preside over a new one—Israel's first television service. The 1968 Independence Day March inaugurated Israel TV and Louis Lentin directed the programme.

Returning to Dublin with Ronit, his Israeli-born wife, he later made the outstanding documentary *Dear Daughter*, an exposé of the abuse of children in Industrial Schools.

Ronit Lentin has in recent years published extensively on migration, inter-culturalism and racism, and co-ordinates the Ethnic and Racial Studies Programme at the Department of Sociology, Trinity College.

Louis Marcus at work on a documentary

Chookie Marcus with her pupils at Stratford College Kindergarten

The Kahan family

1910–1970s

Propped up on a couple of old ledgers, because no chair was high enough for her to reach the oversize Remington typewriter at which she tapped relentlessly, the diminutive Esther Kahan gave no impression of strength. Yet this woman, a Queen Esther of her own, presided in a right royal manner over Dublin's JNF (Jewish National Fund) office in Zion Schools, Bloomfield Avenue, for no less than 30 years. As she hand-cranked her archaic Roneo duplicating machine she would expound her opinions on the leaders of the community; they were short, sharp and consistent.

Esther had two brothers: Robert (Robbie) and Emmanuel (Nouky), both in the Irish Civil Service, who became well-known for widely different reasons.

Robbie, a senior figure in the Office of Public Works, was the confidant of many of the writers of the Irish literary revival period. Fluent in several languages, he was employed as a government censor of mail during the Emergency (Ireland's term for the Second World War); he was also a member of the Irish Jewish Refugee committee. When entrée was needed to government circles, Robbie's help was crucial, as in the case of the establishment of Zion Schools—the first Jewish National School—when the state gave considerable financial assistance for the scheme.

For forty years until his death in 1951, Robbie was the Irish correspondent of the London *Jewish Chronicle*. George Mitofsky, also a community employee and a close friend, groomed Esther to take over the task, which she did until 1979—a remarkable record of one family reporting for a newspaper for a continuous 68 years.

The tale of the other brother, Nouky, is much sadder. One night in 1922 during the Troubles he and a friend had just left the Jewish Club in Harrington Street, Dublin, when they were set upon. Nouky was shot dead and his friend injured, but nobody was ever convicted of the crime. Robbie succeeded in tracking one of the criminals to Moyne Road, but the bird had flown to Australia. Fifty-six years later, Esther still had Nouky's blood-stained wallet in her possession and wept a silent tear as she handed it over for display in the *100 years of Jewish Life in Ireland* exhibition in 1978.

Dr Ellard Eppel

1955–1990s

Dr Ellard Eppel, perhaps one of the last old-fashioned, obliging and much beloved GPs, wore a different *yarmulke* (skull-cap) when addressing Terenure Hebrew Congregation, of which he was President.

He always knew the right thing to say on communal occasions and said it elegantly.

He told a stormy meeting: 'The hall needs redecoration, the toilets need heating, the furniture is fit for a skip, the kitchens are archaic and the caterers are complaining the sinks are not big enough for them.' 'Mr President,' a voice queried from the back, 'has your committee tried getting smaller caterers?'

Past Presidents of the Dublin Jewish Students Union: (back, left–right) Quentin Crivon, Dr Samie Levenson, Dr Ellard Eppel, Dr Neville Boland, Dr Manne Berber, M. Don Buchalter. (front, left–right) Jennie Z. Gilbert, Howard Gross, Marilyn Taylor

James Joyce and Leopold Bloom
1904–1940s

Gerald Davis dressed as Leopold Bloom, the famous Jewish character from Joyce's novel *Ulysses*, on Bloomsday (16th June) *Photograph © Amelia Stein*

Speaking off the cuff, the average person pondering on who was the most famous Dublin Jew might well pass over the Herzogs and the Briscoes and plump for Leopold Bloom, such is the world renowned fame of James Joyce's novel about Bloom, *Ulysses*.

The strange part is that Bloom only existed in Joyce's imagination—'a Jew that never was'—and had he existed, he would never have met the strict conditions required for orthodox Jews: either a Jewish mother or a recognised rabbinical court conversion. The man who set out on his perambulations on 16th June 1904 was uncircumcised, had been baptised three times, and was a Catholic married to a Catholic.

But all this does not deter the coachloads of foreign visitors who turn up to muse over the plaque at 52 Upper Clanbrassil Street, convinced that this was where the great Jew and Irishman was born (although apart from the odd maverick, Jews in fact mainly lived in *Lower* Clanbrassil Street on the other side of the South Circular Road).

Why Joyce chose Dublin Jewry for the background of *Ulysses* is a debate that will never end. At that time Jews constituted the only colourful foreign element of any size in Dublin. Possibly, aware of anti-Semitic rhetoric at the time of the Limerick boycott, Joyce was moved to redress the balance. And of course the image of the Jew as the perennial outsider was and is potent. If Joyce was writing *Ulysses* today, it is fascinating to speculate on the possible nationality of a modern-day Bloom, as there are now so many ethnic groups in Dublin to choose from.

It is believed the author used the 1903 *Thom's Directory* for the names of his Jewish characters—such as Bella Cohen, Israel Citron and the Moiselle family—but flesh on the bones may have been added by Dublin Jewish academic 'Con' Leventhal, an admirer and friend of Joyce (see page 34).

Interestingly, in Joyce's later life, one of his closest friends was a Jew, Paul Léon, who in September 1940 rescued books and papers from Joyce's flat in Paris and delivered them to Count O'Kelly, the Irish ambassador to Nazi-occupied France. Léon was arrested by the Germans, deported and killed by them in 1942.

Gerald Davis, artist and Joycean
1960s–2005

Gerald Davis, genial and much-loved member of the community, was a man of many parts: primarily a painter, but also gallery owner, art collector, jazz enthusiast and sometime businessman.

In 1950 Gerald's father, son of Lithuanian immigrants, set up a stationery shop, the Rubber Stamp Company, in Dublin's Capel Street. Eventually this became the Davis Gallery, where Gerald, always ready to encourage Irish artists, exhibited high-quality craftwork along with contemporary painting and sculpture. In 1995 President Mary Robinson opened a jubilee exhibition showing works by 25 artists.

Gerald first showed his own work in a joint exhibition with Maurice Fridberg, going from strength to strength until in 1987 there was a major 25-year retrospective of his work at the Guinness Hop Store, accompanied by daily lunchtime jazz recitals.

Proud of his Jewish heritage, he described one aspect of it as 'a slight over-the-topness, whether it be playing a violin or telling a joke.'

He had a great interest in James Joyce. And perhaps above all, he will be remembered for, every Bloomsday (16th June), bringing to life the character of Leopold Bloom, the famous Irish Jewish anti-hero of James Joyce's *Ulysses*.

Gerald Davis died in 2005, aged 66.

Gerald Davis in his gallery during his *When I'm Sixty-Four* exhibition, 2002

Henry Barron, Supreme Court Judge—the Barrons and the Bakers

FROM 1930S

Henry Barron's benign countenance belies the sharpness of a mind that has led him to the top rung of the Irish juridical ladder.

Born in Dublin in 1928, Henry is the son of Irish-born descendants of Lithuanian Jewish immigrants. His father, a Captain in the British Army artillery in India during the First World War, was afterwards a railway engineer on the sub-continent; he once recalled how he had been asked to advise on the Bombay, Baroda and Central Indian Railway, known popularly as the BBCI, where on occasion straying cows had right of way over rolling stock.

Qualifying in 1950, Henry was appointed Judge of the High Court in 1982 and to the Supreme Court in 1997, where he served until his retirement three years later. He then presided over the Commission of Investigation into the terrorist bombings which in 1974 took 33 lives and wounded over a hundred in Dublin and Monaghan.

Henry's capacity to become adept at any skill of his choice is much envied by lesser mortals, especially as it is accompanied by such obviously genuine modesty. He has been, by all accounts a major force on the putting green, on the hockey field and at the bridge table; in the Jewish community, he is president of the Irish Jewish Museum.

Henry Barron's late wife, Rosalind, an excellent bridge player herself, and remembered by her friends for her charm and elegance, was the daughter of Leslie Scheps, a Swiss Jewish immigrant to Ireland. Her mother, Sarah Baker, came from a distinguished family of Hebrew educationalists headed by Philip Baker who, as a young Lithuanian immigrant, joined the Sackville Chess Club and quickly became an Irish Grand Master. Owner of a well-known clothing factory, he was renowned in his day as a model employer, liked and respected by all who worked for him, even in hard times. A son, Joshua (Joe) Baker, a distinguished Senior Counsel, lectured at Trinity

College both in Hebrew and as Reid professor of Law.

Of the Barrons' four children, three followed their father into the law and one became an engineer.

Joshua Baker in the 1930s

Judge Henry Barron

Friendly Societies, *B'nai Brith* and BBYO

1900S—PRESENT

The unidentified gentleman in the photograph was a member of the all-male Friendly Society movement which included the Grand Order of Israel and the Order of Ancient Maccabeans. Dressing up in uniform or regalia was a pleasant change from the long humdrum hours of toil.

But the greater advantage of belonging to an Order was that, at a time when social benefits were small or non-existent, a few pence a week would entitle the member to financial help in a crisis. When sick, needing spectacles, dental or medical care, or maybe groceries while 'sitting *shiva*' (the obligatory week's mourning for the passing of close relatives) the few shillings 'relief' was crucial. With the growth of state insurance schemes the Orders lost their *raison d'être*.

An allied, but very different society, founded in 1954, was *B'nai Brith* (Children of the Covenant), a branch of the international order devoted to charitable purposes—and eventually the ladies participated.

In Dublin this outreach group endowed scholarships—open to all—in non-Jewish schools attended by children of the community; Dublin schools Synge Street, Wesley College, Sandford Park and Alexandra College benefited from their fund-raising. Members assisted the Irish Wheelchair Association and the Meals-on-Wheels service in the wider community.

When Charles Stewart Parnell's letters to his mistress (later his wife) Katharine O'Shea, came up for sale, *B'nai Brith* ensured they would not be lost to the Irish nation: they are preserved in Ireland's National Library, Kildare Street.

Still going strong in Dublin is BBYO (the *B'nai Brith* Youth Organisation) which has a programme of meetings, social events, visits to elderly residents of the Jewish Home, and inter-visits with fellow-BBYO members from Britain and further afield. They also raise funds for Irish charities such as MS (multiple sclerosis) and Cystic Fibrosis as well as charities in Israel.

Jewish Friendly Society Member, 1912

Dina Copeman,
Professor of Music

1920S–1970S

Pianist Dina Copeman rose to be senior professor of Dublin's Royal Irish Academy of Music. She played for Radio Éireann's inaugural broadcast and could not resist the odd tinkle on the keys in the Jewish Home where she was later a resident.

When she died in 1978 President Hillery and the entire staff of the RIAM attended the funeral.

Dina Copeman at the piano (above) and in the 1920s (top)

Dahna and Louis Davis, nonagenarian Dublin couple

1900S—PRESENT

Dahna worked in theatre, particularly in the Gas Company Theatre, Dun Laoghaire, and the Busáras Theatre in the basement of Dublin's Bus Station. Louis has a penchant for musical tapes—Irish, Yiddish, Hebrew and classical; he keeps his huge collection in a room to themselves.

They have three daughters, Dr Beatrice Sofaer-Bennett (see page 92), Joyce Shaper, who with her husband Alan is very active in Dublin communal life and in the Irish Zionist movement (see pages 6–8), and Miriam Belman, who now lives in England.

Dahna in 1916, aged seven

Dahna at a reception in the 1950s with famous film star James Mason, who began his career at Dublin's Gate Theatre

Dahna and Louis Davis, 1940

Dahna and Louis Davis today

— 65 —

Immanuel Jakobovits, Chief Rabbi

1949–1959

Appointed in 1949—aged 27—as first Chief Rabbi of the newly created Republic of Ireland, Immanuel Jakobovits was a brilliant though conservative academic, who once said, 'Ireland is 95% Catholic, 5% Protestant; I am Chief Rabbi of the rest.' A man of great learning, he admitted that his greatest asset was his wife, Amelie Munk of Paris—daughter of a prominent rabbi—a young, dynamic woman of great warmth and wisdom. They had six children.

After leaving Ireland in 1958 he became Chief Rabbi of Britain and the Commonwealth, and was elevated to the British House of Lords by the Thatcher government.

His wife, still busy and active in communal life in Britain, is affectionately known by all as 'Lady J'; she, as did her husband, looks back with fondness and nostalgia to the family's years in Ireland.

Chief Rabbi Immanuel Jakobovits (1921–99)

Chief Rabbi Isaac Cohen

Isaac Cohen, Chief Rabbi

1959–1979

A 'Taffy' (Welshman) by birth, Isaac Cohen's mellifluous Welsh accent charmed Irish listeners and viewers when he pioneered the custom of addressing the community's fellow citizens on radio and TV on the Jewish festivals. During his 20 years as Chief Rabbi he consolidated the Jewish community's relations with government and with other religious authorities, and his post was accorded diplomatic status. His wife Fanny contributed qualities of capability, efficiency, good humour and hard work.

The image which particularly caught the public imagination was his lonely figure, pictured in the newspapers in hat and dark suit standing at prayer outside the imposing doors of the Pro Cathedral during the funeral of Éamon de Valera in 1975. (The Jewish religion does not permit *cohanim*, Jewish hereditary priests, to attend funerals.)

(Above) Adelaide Road Synagogue Choir in the late 1930s, flanked on the left by choir-master Philip Modell, and on the right, Cantor Freilich. (In Orthodox synagogues all choirs are solely male.)

(Left) Adelaide Road Synagogue Choir, 1948

Irish team bearing the tricolour at the 6th Maccabiah Games, Israel, 1961

Sport in the community

1908–PRESENT

In the world of sport, the Dublin Jewish community revolved round the main hubs—Edmondstown Golf Club in Rathfarnham, and Maccabi, the now-extinct sports club on Kimmage Road West.

Edmondstown came into existence in 1944 as a Jewish golf club for the simple reason that it was almost impossible for Jews to become members of existing clubs. The nucleus came from the 30 fanatics who formed the Maccabean

Golfing Society and were mad enough to pay £3000 for the 75-acre piece of land in the foothills of the Dublin Mountains.

Today, Edmondstown, with its magnificent facilities, is a far cry from the day when one member would purloin lost balls and the next day, chip them from the quays into the Liffey. The ethnic composition of the membership is no longer exclusively Jewish for two reasons—fewer Jewish golfers around, and also in the more liberal climate of the 21st century, the exclusion of non-Jewish players would be considered illegal due to equality laws!

The origin of Maccabi Sports Club was in the Carlisle Cricket Club founded in 1908—so named after a street in Little Jerusalem (Portobello) where it was conceived. Some of the players were non-Jewish and youths of both religions often faced parental problems when playing on their Sabbaths—the Jews on Saturdays and the Christians on Sundays.

The founders, 'Acky' Hesselberg and his mates, would conceal cricket gear about their persons until they arrived at the match venue, thus hoping to hide the real purpose of an afternoon's quiet stroll.

Captains two: Joan and John Finkel, Captain and Lady Captain, at Edmondstown Golf Club, 1987, with the late Stanley Adams, long-time secretary manager of the club

Tony Leon, auctioneer, wearing his other hat as enthusiastic Maccabi cricketer, 1967

Maccabi Women's Tennis Team 1959. Back row (left–right) Vivien Waterman (née Lee), Edith Jacobs (née Robinson), Rhoda Davis (née Wine). Front row (left–right) Seva Solomons (née Miller), Juliet Eppel (née Shenkman), Helen Roberts (née Hool)

Billy Noyk, son of lawyer and national activist Michael Noyk, playing polo in the Phoenix Park, 1960s

The Carlisle Rugby Club was founded two years later and by 1918 the Carlisle Athletic Union was based in Green Lane, Kimmage, later in Parkmore Drive. Its final and finest home was in Kimmage Road West, where Dublin Maccabi opened its gates in 1954; it boasted 1,000 members, adults and children, with rugby, tennis, soccer, wrestling, boxing, table tennis and judo sections. There were dances, social and cultural activities and a café where young couples could gaze at each other over an inexpensive cup of coffee.

Among the successes of Maccabi was its cricket team. An American rabbi visiting the sports ground noted Rodney Molins in his white umpire's coat. He explained to his wife, 'He's a doctor and he is here in case anybody gets injured.' Molins became an International Selector for Ireland, and it seems cricket is in the family genes. His nephew Jason, captain of the Irish cricket team, and Jason's brother were jointly selected; so was his cousin, Lara, for the Irish Ladies International Cricket Team. Mark Cohen also had a distinguished career in the

sport as did Sonny Hool, Louis Jacobson and Mervyn Jaffey when they were 'Gentlemen of Ireland' and cricket was cricket.

But soon the halcyon days were over and as the Jewish population shrank, so did Maccabi's membership. (When by 1999 it had decreased to 100, the Club was sold to millionaire Ben Dunne for around £4 million.)

In 1987, in appreciation of the Jewish community's involvement with sport, Judge Hubert Wine, a table tennis International, was approached to hold the

Maccabi Cricket Team 1952

'Gift of Sport' service in Adelaide Road Synagogue—a State occasion, attended by the President of Ireland and State dignitaries.

Not to be omitted from the list are the chess players, and of course, the *kurtan spielers* (Yiddish for card players). Card games have always been popular with Jews; poker, pontoon, whist and bridge were the favourites. Bridge has produced Irish Internationals and gifted players from the Jewish community including Don and Barbara Seligman, Adam Mesbur, David Jackson, Harry Fine, Marcus Shrage and Frank Fine—a seven-trick Grand Slam!

In September 2006, under non-playing captain David Jackson, the Irish team returned home from the European Bridge Championships in Warsaw with a silver medal.

Junior Tennis at Maccabi, 1956: Edmund Ross (left) and Derek Wine

Members of the Scouting movement at the 1959 youth parade in Adelaide Road

Lorraine, Fiona and Marian Brattman 1981—the only time three sisters were in the Brownies together

Scouts and Guides
1929–PRESENT

There has been a Jewish Scout movement in Dublin for 80 years. George Morris, a founder-member and the first Scoutmaster, attended the first jamboree in Cheshire in 1929. Maurie Gordon, who became Scoutmaster in 1936, was also a key guiding force. The Scouts, Cubs, Guides and Brownies flourished and also participated in wider Irish Scout and Guide movements.

The Ireland–Israel Friendship League

1967–PRESENT

At the beginning of 1967, when it looked as though the State of Israel was in dire danger of being wiped off the map, Gabriel Fallon, former Abbey actor and later theatre critic, along with Jennie Z. Gilbert of the Jewish community, launched the Ireland–Israel Friendship League, inviting Cearbhall Ó Dálaigh to become its first patron. Ó Dálaigh, whose multi-faceted qualifications would have made him successful in half-a-dozen careers, and who later became President of Ireland, responded, 'It will be an honour to lend a hand.'

The early meetings of the League in Dublin's Buswell's Hotel were characterised by large attendances, especially as the traumatic atmosphere of the Six Day War seized the public's attention. At meetings the front row was often occupied by not-so-young ladies listening avidly to the handsome Gabriel's dulcet tones.

A later chairman, Adele Darlington, had learned Hebrew from a DIY (Do It Yourself) book, and in her widowhood she 'made Aliyah' (immigrated) to Israel where she married a German-Jewish refugee and lived in Jerusalem.

The League, of course, consisted of both Jewish and non-Jewish members and its panel of speakers attracted many prominent personalities. Jennie Z. Gilbert, Public Relations Officer for many years, had the magic quality of waving her wand at potential speakers,

Prime Minister of Israel Benjamin Netanyahu (left), Israeli Ambassador to Ireland Zvi Gabay and Brian Quinn, President of the Ireland–Israel Friendship League, 1996

leaving them no option but to agree to address the League.

Another outstanding patron was Professor Lochlainn O'Raifeartaigh, whose modest demeanour concealed a renowned scientist who came to the Ireland–Israel League by way of discussions with Jewish European colleagues.

For many years meetings took place in the Leslie Golding Hall at Adelaide Road Synagogue, later in the Dublin Jewish Progressive and currently in Terenure Synagogues. When Brian Quinn retired from a successful career as a journalist, he was told, 'Now that you have nothing

to do, what about becoming chairman of the Ireland–Israel Friendship League?' Brian accepted the challenge with grace, carrying out his duties in an incomparable manner until 2003. And who can forget the professional way his wife Alice, with helpers, made sure the cup of tea was ready for the members once the meeting was over.

The present chairman is Oliver Donohoe—also a member of the Holocaust Educational Trust of Ireland—who strongly believes in the necessity of the League as a bridge between Ireland and Israel. Formerly a producer with RTÉ (Irish Television), he worked on the prestigious *Late Late Show*. He went on to ICTU (Irish Congress of Trade Unions) where he specialised in education, information and communications. He is presently on the National Council for Curriculum Assessment.

Over the years the League has done Trojan work in explaining the complexities of Israel's remarkable history and its ongoing precarious existence surrounded by enemies sworn to its destruction, while also deepening the links with Ireland, another small country with a complex history.

Community protest on behalf of Russian refuseniks outside the Soviet embassy Dublin 1970s. Some of the protestors wore striped prison garb of the notorious Russian Gulag.

Jacqueline Tolkin of the Irish Soviet Jewry Committee with Yitzhak Rabin, later Defence Minister and Prime Minister of Israel

The 35s and Soviet Jewry: 'Let My People Go!'
1970s

The Rathmines cabbie recounted with surprise his recent experience on the Orwell Road, Dublin where, he said, 'Jewish young wans and oul' wans were paradin' in their PJs (pyjamas), and the guards (Irish police) were after them keeping an eye out.'

It was the 1970s and remarkably, the story was true. The banner-carrying ladies of the 35s, assisted by male supporters, were protesting outside the embassy of the then Soviet Union seeking the right for Jews to emigrate to Israel from Russia, where due to repression and anti-Semitism their lives were intolerable and sometimes in mortal danger. These frustrated asylum-seekers—refuseniks—were often inmates of the Gulag, a network of harsh Russian prison camps where their striped uniforms were similar to the pyjamas bought from Clery's store in Dublin and worn by the demonstrators. The protesters were watched over by the police who gently ensured they kept moving.

The 35s originated in the appearance in a Moscow street of a fearless Jewish woman of that age carrying a banner inscribed 'Let My People Go!' This courageous act in a cruel police state inspired 35s groups in Europe, including Dublin, where there was already an Irish Soviet Jewry Committee established by Jacqueline Tolkin and Rochelle Baker.

When Soviet artists performed in Dublin, the 35s were outside presenting white roses and a card asking theatregoers to remember the refuseniks, who were prevented from leaving Russia.

The 35s, as well as members of the Soviet Jewry Committee, which included Alan Shatter, Alan Benson, Carol Danker and Alan Eppel, made clandestine trips to the Soviet Union bringing 'illegal' goodies such as prayer books, chocolate, and clothes. The group was chaired for many years by Lynn Jackson, until the dissolution of the Soviet Union ended the ban on emigration. Now the Irish National Council for Soviet Jewry helps Russian Jewish immigrants settle in Israel.

The movement in Dublin attracted notable non-Jewish sympathisers, including Ruairi Quinn—later Labour Party leader—and Sister Stanislaus, religious activist; people of all religions and politics often joined the demonstrators.

Martin Bates of the Irish army, a fluent Russian speaker, willingly gave up hours of his free time to translate phone messages of solidarity to and from refuseniks.

The movement never let the issue drop from sight. With *glasnost* (the thaw) most refuseniks were eventually allowed to emigrate. Jewish emigration from Russia still continues.

With President Chaim Herzog giving a presentation from the Ireland-Israel Friendship League.

Jennie Z making a presentation to President Chaim Herzog on behalf of the Ireland–Israel Friendship League, 1987

Jennie Z. Gilbert, Zionist and community activist
1930S—EARLY 1980S

Jennie Gilbert, née Rubenstein, popularly known as 'Jennie Z', was especially famous for the astonishing number of Presidential hats she wore—and no wonder, as she had won a gold medal for 'Impromptu' speaking at the Solicitors' Apprentices Debating Society. Although she did not pursue a legal career, in 1969 she was the first Irish grandmother to be called to the Bar.

Earlier, as an accomplished violinist, she was not above playing at the weekly shilling dances in Greenville Hall where young Jewish Romeos tangoed the nights away with their young ladies.

Jennie became a member of the International Committee of the Irish Housewives' Association, and in 1967, with Abbey actor and drama critic

Gabriel Fallon, helped to found the Ireland–Israel Friendship League; she served this organisation—still going strong—for many years as PRO and in other capacities.

Jennie Z was married to Gerald Gilbert of the eponymous firm of estate agents; he was also an outstanding voluntary worker for the Irish Jewish community.

'The Freedman Boys' in the 1950s: Louis (left) was a founder member of Greenville Hall Synagogue and prominent in the Board of Guardians, and his brother Wolfe was a founder member of Terenure Synagogue and also Chairman of the Zionist Council. Among their grand-children is Derek Freedman MD, one of Ireland's leading authorities on sexually transmitted infections.

Hilda White (née Fine) in her kosher Terenure grocery shop (1980s). You could die for Hilda's home-pickled garlic cucumbers, each one a meal in itself.

The Jewish Home

1950S—PRESENT

The Jewish Home is over 50 years old, and caters for the elderly of the whole island. It has recently moved from Rathmines to fine new accommodation, Bloomfield, in Stocking Lane (founded by the Quaker movement), in the Dublin mountains.

Residents in the garden of the Jewish Home, Denmark Hill

The Jewish Home, Denmark Hill, 1980

Percy Diamond of the Jewish Home, singing *c.*1980

Baila in her Clanbrassil Street shop in the 1980s

Baila Erlich, kosher butcher

1950s–1990s

It could truly be said that Baila Erlich was born into the kosher butchery business, because even in her early days, old people recounted seeing her as a child, helping her father to eke out a meagre livelihood.

Baila's name appears in the rolls of Zion Schools, Bloomfield Avenue in the 1930s, and as soon as she could, she joined the family business, which in 1952 was relocated to 35 Lower Clanbrassil Street in the heart of Little Jerusalem.

Twenty years later on the death of her father, Baila took charge, with nobody left in doubt of her supremacy in her little domain. She was a small woman with as biting a tongue as a garlic-pickled cucumber, and an outward barbed disregard for all and sundry, disguising her deep compassion for the needy with an exasperating take-it-or-leave-it attitude.

As well as those individual cases of all faiths to whose needs she responded, the 'touchers' on the way home from the local would find her easy meat in terms of donations in kind. Baila's discreet contributions to charitable organisations will never be recorded and that is the way she would have wished it to be.

Her accounting system belied the necessity for computers. Purchases and orders were recorded on scraps of cardboard and dropped into the deep pockets of an enfolding crossover pinafore. These, presumably, were eventually translated into accounts. What her Muslim customers made of this—they bought from Baila before they had their own Halal shops—is anybody's guess!

The shop, Erlich's, which later also sold groceries, was the last kosher provisions shop left in Clanbrassil Street, and when Baila died in 1997, it died with her. The Jewish Representative Council tried to run it until 2001, but there could be no Erlich's without Baila, the fierce little woman who once had the temerity to loudly criticise Chief Rabbi David Rosen when she learned that he and his family were confirmed vegetarians.

The staff was a mixture of Jews and non-Jews. One Catholic butcher served with the firm for over 50 years and knew all there was to be known about *Kashrut* (Kosher food). Two of the Catholic elderly 'girls' worked away in Baila's kitchen making Jewish delicacies for sale which brought back the taste of food as it was in Baila's grandmother's day.

June Levine, feminist
1970s–1990s

June Levine was born in Dublin and will be long remembered by Irish women as a staunch member of the group who fought a pioneering battle for women's liberation in Ireland in the 1970s. In her best-selling book *Sisters*, a personal history of the Irish feminist movement, she wrote: 'the whole world, for women, was occupied country'. The book is considered seminal by those interested in feminism in Ireland.

A later book, *Lyn: A Story of Prostitution* (1987), which June Levine wrote with Lyn Madden who worked for 20 years as a prostitute, has become a classic and remains as compelling as ever, providing a stark insight into life 'on the game' in Dublin.

Later, in a collection of oral histories, June Levine vividly described her contradictory childhood. Daughter of a Catholic mother and a Jewish father, she alternated between attending church and synagogue, and between the two sets of grandparents, both affectionate, but utterly different in their lives and attitudes.

June Levine lives in Dublin and, according to her friend, journalist and writer Mary Kenny, although June once said that marriage was an institution invented by the patriarchy to keep women down, 'she is today not only married, but maintains one of the most beautiful homes and the most delightful tables I know'.

June Levine

Cearbhall Ó Dálaigh

President Cearbhall Ó Dálaigh and the Jews
1960s–1970s

In 1974 when Cearbhall Ó Dálaigh, a former Chief Justice of the Supreme Court, was elected President of Ireland, it turned out to be a landmark for the small Jewish community.

On the evening of his inauguration he attended a celebratory service in the Adelaide Road Synagogue—the first to attend in person, rather than sending a representative, a precedent which was then followed by all subsequent Presidents.

His contacts with the community were said to go back to his early childhood when he acted as a *Shabbos goy*—a friendly non-Jewish neighbour who would switch lights on and off and light fires for orthodox Jews forbidden to do these chores on the Sabbath.

Later the President wished to invite the then Chief Rabbi to Áras an Uachtaráin (his official residence), but of course there was the problem of kosher refreshments. Undaunted, he travelled personally to Bretzel's (the kosher bakery) for approved bread, and Rubenstein's (kosher butcher) for salt beef.

So, at the Áras, buttered salt beef sandwiches were served to Chief Rabbi Isaac Cohen—the chef not realising that the mixing of milk and meat substances is strictly forbidden by the laws of *Kashrut!*

In 1967 President Ó Dálaigh became the first patron of the newly formed Ireland–Israel Friendship League headed by Gabriel Fallon, an honour of which the President remained extremely proud.

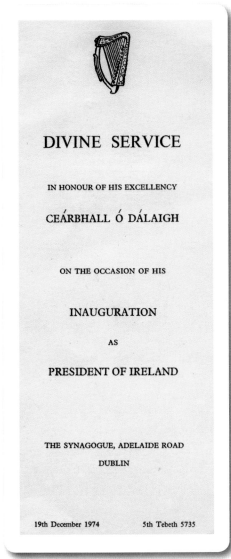

Order of Service at Adelaide Road Synagogue marking Cearbhall Ó Dálaigh's accession to the Presidency

The Currid bequest
1980s

A casual visitor to the small, then ultra-orthodox *Machzikei Hadass* Synagogue at 77 Terenure Road North might have been astonished to witness a memorial service for a Catholic showman who died in 1983.

As a very young man, inviting people to 'Roll or bowl a penny a pitch', John Currid worked the Dublin fairgrounds, but when it came to prizes for successful punters, his resources were limited. No one would extend credit except a couple of Jewish wholesalers, such as Freedman's and Lewis's, who came to his rescue with tea sets, teddy bears, umbrellas or holy pictures.

With the passage of years Currid became a Dublin property owner whose portfolio included a town centre amusement arcade.

When the entrepreneur made his will he left bequests to many charities, and directed that the balance of his estate should go to the Dublin Jewish Board of Guardians. Over £600,000 accrued to the Board, enabling it to conduct its charitable donations to those fallen on hard times with greater generosity.

John Currid's request that he be remembered in their prayers is honoured annually by the Jewish congregations of Dublin.

Interior of the Machzikei Hadass Synagogue, Terenure Road North, a small congregation, successor to St Kevin's Parade, which was established in 1883, and moved to Terenure in 1967

International Conference of Jewish Media, Jerusalem 1986. Keynote speaker Dr Conor Cruise O'Brien (second from left), pictured here with the Dublin delegation, Barbara Cohen (left), Asher Benson and Marilyn Taylor, received a standing ovation.

The Loyal League of Yiddish Sons of Erin, New York, in 1975—an expatriate group of Irish Jews whose bagels were dyed green for St Patrick's Day

Raphael Siev, curator, Irish Jewish Museum, and his brother Asher (Stanley) Siev, lawyer

LATE 1970S—PRESENT

Raphael Siev, Curator, Irish Jewish Museum, Walworth Road, 2007

When Dubliner Raphael Siev became the curator of the Irish Jewish Museum, he was embarking on a second career, and embraced this new but honorary appointment as enthusiastically as the first.

A lawyer in the Land Registry, he transferred to the Department of Foreign Affairs and the Diplomatic Corps.

Educated in Dublin and at *yeshiva* (religious school) in Gateshead, England, he became a Senior Counsel, and when Ireland acceded to the Common Market (later to become the EU), he attended as Ireland's representative at legal 'gigs' all over Europe and North America.

Albert (Raphael's father) was born on a Russian roadside, and his mother died in childbirth as they were escaping from the anti-Semitism of Eastern Europe. Eventually Albert arrived in Ireland, prospered, but never gave up his bicycle, which he rode like a fiery steed!

Raphael's brother Asher attended The High School—then in Harcourt Street—and as well as educational classes he 'enjoyed boxing and rugby and played as a forward in the school team from 1935 to 1939'—the only Jewish pupil in the team. He later became a well-known Dublin lawyer and the first Irish Jewish notary.

Asher Siev (centre back) in the High School Rugby team, 1936–7

Asher Siev blowing the traditional shofar (ram's horn)

— 84 —

The Walworth Road Synagogue, of which Albert was a trustee, closed in 1970 through lack of attendance. Following his son Asher's suggestion that the synagogue should be turned into a museum, steps were taken to set up the new institution. When the museum committee was set up in 1984, the Siev family endowed the building in the name of their late mother, Edith.

Raphael's diplomatic career took him to Copenhagen, where he was Deputy Head of Mission in the Irish Embassy. He had a narrow escape when, having got the local Jewish community's permission to park his car in their compound, terrorists blew up the gates, narrowly missing him.

As he contentedly lectures in the museum to groups ranging from children to senior citizens, and to visitors from all over the world, it may seem a far cry from his days at the United Nations when he sat, in the alphabetical order adopted by the UN, between Iraq and Israel—but the smile on his face indicates how much he is enjoying his second life.

Three Faiths Forum

1997–PRESENT

The Three Faiths Forum of Ireland had its inaugural meeting in September 1997. The group includes the Imams of the Sunni and Shiah mosques, and representatives of the Jewish community, the Catholic Church, the Church of Ireland, the Presbyterian Church and the Irish School of Ecumenics. The group still meets on a regular basis.

Christian Friends of Israel in Ireland

1980S–PRESENT

Sister Carmel Niland (second from right) with two members of her Order (left); Sir Sigmund Sternberg, National President of the World Council of Christians and Jews, and Debbie Briscoe (right) of the Irish Council of Christians and Jews, arriving to visit President Mary Robinson at Áras an Uachtaráin, 1996

Paddy Monaghan is an energetic leading light in the Irish Christian Friends of Israel, 'a group of Christians who accept the biblical truth that God gave the land of Israel to the Jewish people forever'. They pray for Israel, remind Christians of their Jewish roots and strengthen Irish–Jewish relationships.

To this end the Christian Friends encourage their members to visit Israel and they have participated in joint Irish Jewish–Christian solidarity tours, a highlight of which is a visit to the Ireland Peace and Reconciliation Forest near Jerusalem. The Forest is supported by the Irish government, the Christian churches and the Irish Council of Christians and Jews.

The Friends work closely with the International Christian Embassy Jerusalem, whose branches worldwide 'bring comfort to the Jewish people'. The Irish group has successfully helped to bring 40,000 Jews from the former USSR to Israel.

Every year Paddy Monaghan and friends arrange a *neshef* (party) to celebrate Israel's Independence Day with a Hebrew song, a dance, a prayer and a bit of Israeli 'nosh'. The atmosphere is charged with the sincerity the Christian Friends feel for Israel.

To foster dialogue between the two faiths, the Irish Council of Christians and Jews, with religious and lay members, was founded 25 years ago. The Council, of which Chief Rabbi David Rosen was a founder member, arranges public meetings for visiting speakers.

Sister Carmel Niland, secretary of the Council, is also a member of the Sisters of Our Lady of Sion, a French order established 40 years ago in the wake of Vatican II. Their worldwide groups are devoted to strengthening Christian–Jewish relationships and breaking down prejudice. Their charming house in Bellinter, Co. Meath—recently sold—contained an excellent library of Judaica.

The Irish School of Ecumenics at Milltown Park also promotes joint Christian–Jewish educational projects.

Chief Rabbi David Rosen

David Rosen, Chief Rabbi
1979–1985

Endowed with a photographic memory, superb PR skills, a sense of humour, and the ability to draw answers from his finger tips, David Rosen was the darling of the Irish media, especially as he had Irish Jewish ancestry, and not least, a charming and intelligent wife, Sharon and three daughters, the youngest Irish-born.

Rabbi Rosen came to Ireland following a term in Capetown, South Africa where he had managed to play a positive role in the fight against apartheid. His period of office here was marked by a reaching out and drawing in both of those in the Jewish community, and of the wider community, and is remembered for the many joyous religious and social activities.

He was devoted to the cause of making the community 'more vibrant and leaner' and to promoting interfaith friendship between Jews and Christians.

Founder of the Irish Council of Christians and Jews, his subsequent success in the promotion of Catholic-Jewish relations on an international level was acknowledged when in 2005 he was made a papal Knight Commander of the Order of St Gregory at a ceremony in Jerusalem, a rare honour for a Jew. This occasion was marked by a celebration in Terenure Synagogue attended by religious leaders, including Archbishop of Dublin Diarmuid Martin, dignitaries and numerous friends of the Rosen family.

Now living with his family in Israel, Rabbi Rosen is Director of the Department of Inter-Religious Affairs of the American Jewish Committee in New York. He is an International President of the World Conference of Religions for Peace—incorporating 15 religions in over 50 countries—and an Honorary President of the International Council of Christians and Jews. He also serves as a member of the Executive Committee of the World Congress of Imams and Rabbis.

Ireland's favourite comedienne Maureen Potter being presented with an illuminated address by Dublin Jewish actor Gerry Alexander. He graduated from the Dublin Jewish Dramatic Society, and appeared at the Abbey Theatre, in films, on radio and TV in the 1960s and 1970s.

Maurice Fridberg (centre), Clare Street publisher of the Hourglass Library and Irish cookery books; he also photographed fascinating images of trees. He and his wife Audrey (right) toiled for the less fortunate members of the community. Pictured left is Dr Samie Levenson, Scottish GP with a surgery in the South Circular Road, who, despite his many years in Dublin, never lost his strong Glaswegian accent.

Jews in Irish politics

1980—PRESENT

Dr Hazel Boland, née Ross

Ireland's 1981 general election was a watershed in the history of Dublin's Jewish community, for no less than four Jewish candidates presented themselves for election to the Dáil (Irish Parliament). The result: three men took seats; the woman failed in her efforts.

She was Dubliner Dr Hazel Boland (née Ross), a Mount Merrion GP (general practitioner) married to Stanley, another dashing GP who on the sports front was also an avid follower of the hunt. Hazel was a hard worker with a fine record of voluntary service, especially in 1977–9 as Chairperson of the Council for the Status of Women (later the National Women's Council of Ireland).

In the Jewish community she was a stylish, memorable figure; she chaired the Regional Council of Women Zionists and the Zionist Council of Ireland.

Her defeat at the polls was disappointing, as she had been supported by the then Taoiseach (Prime Minister) himself, Charles Haughey. Electoral office eluded her; both Stanley and Hazel died before their time.

Ben Briscoe (see *The Briscoe family*, page 24) was re-elected as he had been several times since 1965. The two 'new boys', Mervyn Taylor (Labour Party) and Alan Shatter (Fine Gael) were both Dublin solicitors, and for the next twenty years or so all three were returned as TDs.

Ben Briscoe, former TD

Mervyn Taylor, born 1931, worked as a young lawyer for Herman Good, who had once stood unsuccessfully for the Irish Labour Party. Taylor's father-in-law Lord Fisher, father of his wife Marilyn, was Mayor of Camden in North London and later became a Labour life peer. Taylor himself also started at local government level representing the growing new town of Tallaght in South West Dublin, and rose rapidly to become Chairman of Dublin County Council, and later Chairman of the Labour Party.

In the Dáil he became the first Jew to occupy a Cabinet post, that of Minister of the newly created Department of Equality and Law Reform. He was responsible for much reforming legislation, especially in the areas of minority rights, women's rights and family law. In 1995 he led a successful campaign in the constitutional

Mervyn Taylor, former TD and Government Minister, addressing the Council of Europe 1985

for the under-privileged expressed itself in Private Members' Bills, especially in the areas of health, welfare and justice, some of which were eventually adopted into law. He also successfully lobbied for the formation of an Oireachtas (Government) Committee on Foreign Affairs, of which he was chairman. He is a former President of the Irish Council against Blood Sports.

All three TDs were staunch defenders of the State of Israel, in whose defence they were never found wanting. They battled for Russian Jewish refuseniks then denied the right to emigrate from the USSR (see page 74), and they still found time to help in the running of the Jewish community.

In the course of an interview in 1981 Taylor said: 'Jewishness was never an issue.' But in the Dáil on one occasion Shatter was needled with anti-Semitic remarks and told, 'Go back where you came from', although muted apologies were made afterwards.

In 2002 Shatter lost his seat, but won it back at the next election in 2007.

Alan Shatter, TD

referendum to allow the introduction of divorce in Ireland, previously not permitted in this country of strong Catholic faith.

Taylor has now retired but is still surrounded by the law: his two sons are lawyers and his daughter is married to one. However his renegade wife Marilyn (née Fisher) is a successful writer of books, some of Jewish interest, for young teenagers.

The third TD Alan Shatter, born 1951, developed a strong interest in Irish family law on which he became an acknowledged expert at an early age. His book *Family Law in the Republic of Ireland* was published in 1977 and ran to several editions. He was in local government prior to 1981, and in the Dáil his concern

Hubert Wine, Judge

1930s–1990s

As Hubert Wine sat in Adelaide Road Synagogue's wooden box seats (reserved for dignitaries) one day in 1999 he reflected on the de-consecration of the building. The 107-year-old lady was coming to her end as a place of worship, victim of the sharply declining number of Dublin Jews; the grand interior would be seen no more, neither would the initials carved into the benches by bored little boys, now long dead.

Hubert was first brought to the *shul* (synagogue) in 1926 at the age of four; since then he had been a regular attender, as had his father and grandfather before him. He first joined Adelaide's Council in 1949, and as the portals closed he had ended up as Honorary Life President. During his time in office he hosted a weekly *Kiddush* (blessing after Sabbath morning prayers) in his Ranelagh home to which selected guests were invited to drink a '*L'Chaim*' ('To Life!'—a traditional toast).

In the community he was also involved with the Jewish Representative Council and served two seven-year stints as chairman.

In his 'civilian' career Hubert chose not to enter the family business—the renowned 'Wine's Antiques' of Grafton Street—but instead opted for law. He worked with Herman Good, but soon branched out on his own, specialising in criminal law and conveyancing.

Judge Hubert Wine, with Cynthia Baker

When he was appointed a judge at Rathfarnham District Court, and later at Dun Laoghaire, he sat when necessary on Sunday, rather than the Sabbath. Very concerned about 'the law's delay' he once held court in his room in the Blackrock Clinic where he was recovering from an operation.

In Dublin's legal history Hubert will probably be remembered for a *cause célèbre* in 1990, when he took a firm stand by refusing to remand a disturbed 15-year-old girl to Mountjoy Prison: instead, the judge said, she should go to a more suitable detention centre, which, it turned out, did not exist in Ireland. The ensuing furore involved the Taoiseach (Prime Minister) Charles Haughey, and it was eventually directed that a house be provided for the girl, who in the meantime had attempted suicide, and that social and medical services be provided for her.

The DPP (Director of Public Prosecutions) withdrew charges against the girl, and Hubert had won this particular battle for the weak and disadvantaged. He commented, 'Even if it were for one little soul saved, it was worth it.'

Chief Rabbi Ephraim Mirvis ('Man of the Match') playing cricket with well-known all-round sportsman Louis Jay, 1980s

Ephraim Mirvis, Chief Rabbi

1984–1992

Of South African origin, Ephraim Mirvis and his wife Valerie had a particular interest in Jewish education, which he described as 'the key to the survival of the Jewish people'. In 1989 Stratford College, whose educational system he consolidated, received the much-coveted Jerusalem prize for Torah education outside Israel.

Early in his term, Rabbi Mirvis led a successful appeal to the Irish government to prevent Pieter Menten, a notorious, newly released Nazi war criminal, from coming to live in a house he owned in Waterford.

Remembered with much fondness in Ireland for his knowledge, kindness and humility, he now lives in North London where he is minister of a prestigious syna-gogue; his wife Valerie has published a successful book on caring and empathising with patients.

A keen follower of the fortunes of Ireland's football team, he still attends their matches whenever possible. And in case he lets his allegiance waver, he now has four 'Paddy' sons to keep him on the straight and narrow.

Beatrice Sofaer-Bennett (née Davis) was awarded a PhD from the University of Edinburgh in 1984 for her work on pain relief. She completed her post-doctoral studies at The Hebrew University Jerusalem.

Refugee from Nazi Europe Serge Philipson's chequered career spanned mining to manufacturing to patron of the arts and to Officier of the Légion d'Honneur (awarded for his services to Irish–French relations). Pictured outside the National Gallery, Dublin 1970s.

Born in Dublin in 1915, Rev. Abraham Gittleson was Minister at Greenville Hall Synagogue and trained as a *mohel* to perform ritual circumcisions. With the help of his loyal and hard-working wife he devoted his life to the community, and on his death in 1984 his memory was honoured by a fund in his name for pupils of Jewish studies at Stratford College.

Rabbi Jacqueline Tabick

CONTEMPORARY

Blonde baby Jackie was born in 1948 to Daisy and Ivor Acker, who lived in Fortfield Park on Dublin's south side. Her parents, among the first to be engaged in the export business, posted food parcels to Britain where there were still acute shortages as a result of the Second World War.

Who could foretell in the early 1950s that this baby girl would sprout a BA Honours degree specialising in medieval history, before embarking on a rabbinical course in London's Leo Baeck College? The ground was truly broken in 1975 when she became the first woman in these islands to become a rabbi. Currently she is the rabbi of North West Surrey Reform Synagogue.

Jackie is strong on interfaith and social justice matters, broadcasts on radio and appears on television, where she is a regular on the *Pause for Thought* programme. As if this is not enough, she writes articles for educational and Jewish magazines and has contributed to publications by the British Women Rabbis' Group. She is chair of the World Congress of Faiths and vice-president of the Reform Movement.

As far as marriage is concerned, it is a tale of two rabbis, because her husband, Brooklyn-born Larry Tabick is also a Reform Synagogue rabbi, and they have three children.

'Uncle Arthur' (Guinness) never attended Hebrew classes, but as the label on the bottle indicates, he was a polyglot as well as a malt expert (2001).

The over-80s group, pictured in 2004, who met to vie with each other while reminiscing over cups of tea. (Left–right) Nick Harris, Louis Davis, Jack Roberts, Dr Ellard Eppel, Geoffrey Phillips

Lighting Sabbath candles, Dublin, 1980s

Commemorating the Holocaust in Ireland

1995–PRESENT

by LYNN JACKSON

Yom Hashoah (Holocaust Memorial Day) is marked by the Irish Jewish community every year. In 1995, through the initiative of Paddy Fitzgibbon of the Rotary Club of Listowel, a public monument was erected to the victims of the Holocaust in The Garden of Europe, Listowel, Co. Kerry.

Ireland became a signatory in Stockholm at the International Forum on the Holocaust in the year 2000, at which signatory nations committed themselves to commemorating and teaching about the Holocaust every year. January 27th—the date Auschwitz–Birkenau was liberated in 1945—was designated Holocaust Memorial Day.

In Ireland, the national Holocaust Memorial Day commemoration takes place on the Sunday nearest to that date every year. The first HMD commemoration took place in 2003. The event is organised by an ad hoc committee of volunteers in association with the Department of Justice, Equality and Law Reform. The commemoration recalls the persecution and annihilation of millions of innocent men, women and children who were murdered by the Nazis.

Ireland has set a precedent by commemorating all of the victims of the Holocaust, persecuted because of their ethnicity, ability, sexual orientation, political convictions or their faith.

The launch of the Holocaust Educational Trust of Ireland in September 2005. (Left–right) Tom O'Higgins, Sister Carmel Niland, Ruairi Quinn, President Mary McAleese, Lynn Jackson, Oliver Donohoe, Barry Andrews.

Belsen survivors Tomi Reichental and the late Terry Samuels

The theme of the commemoration is *Learning from the past—lessons for today.* The ceremony takes the form of readings, survivors' recollections, music and candle-lighting. The President of Ireland and the Taoiseach have participated in the commemoration. It is attended by people from all walks of Irish life and it is a very moving, dignified and impressive occasion.

The Holocaust Educational Trust of Ireland was established in 2005 and launched by the President of Ireland. The Trust aims to educate and inform about the Holocaust in order to combat anti-Semitism and all forms of racism and intolerance in Ireland. The founding trustees are drawn from the political, religious, educational and philanthropic spheres of Irish society. The Trust is chaired by Ruairi Quinn TD.

HETI designs educational programmes and cultural projects for all school levels and for the general public.

Lynn Jackson is founder and chief executive of the Holocaust Educational Trust of Ireland, a member of the Holocaust Memorial Day Committee and former chairperson of the Irish Council for Soviet Jewry.

Lynn Jackson, 1980s founder of the Holocaust Educational Trust of Ireland

Yaakov Pearlman, Chief Rabbi

FROM 2001

Of course, nobody who is anybody is devoid of Irish ancestry, and when the present Chief Rabbi of Ireland, Manchester-born Dr Yaakov Pearlman—who had served congregations for a number of years in the US—took office in Dublin, it came as no surprise that 100 years ago his Hyamson grandparents lived here.

Having antecedents from the *Heim* (the old country) living in the centre of Little Jerusalem is surely as prestigious as an American being in direct line with the

The induction of Ireland's new Chief Rabbi Yaakov Pearlman in 2001. (Left–right) Michael Gilbert (Terenure Synagogue), UK Chief Rabbi Sir Jonathan Sacks, Stephen Molins (Jewish Representative Council), President of Ireland Mary McAleese, Alan Benson (then President Representative Council), Chief Rabbi Pearlman, Judge Hubert Wine (Adelaide Road Synagogue).

Chief Rabbi Pearlman with Taoiseach (Prime Minister) Bertie Ahern at the Irish Jewish Museum 2005

Estelle Menton (1980s): Chair of the Irish Council for Soviet Jewry, and later first woman Chair of the Irish Jewish Representative Council

Pilgrim Fathers who sailed to America on the Mayflower (if the Rabbi will forgive the comparison!).

Dr Pearlman is a 'people person' who, with his friendly demeanour, has maintained the high standards of the Irish Chief Rabbinate. During his time here, among many other achievements he has greatly extended the range of kosher food available.

In his work he has an able partner, his wife Dr Sheila Pearlman, an academic specialising in education and mathematics, who uses her skills in many ways, giving unstinting help at the Irish Jewish Museum and Stratford College; she also works with a group on the preservation of the old Jewish cemetery in Limerick.

Despite all this activity she still finds time to deliver programmes of talks on aspects of Jewish history and belief to the community, to help out on an occasional Shabbaton (communal celebration of the Sabbath) and frequently visit the residents at the Jewish Home.

Dayan (rabbinical judge) Zalman Alony, c.1975, minister to the Dublin Jewish community for many years

Rabbi Zalman Lent
CONTEMPORARY

One night in December, outside the Mansion House, Dublin, a little boy pulled at his mother's sleeve. 'There's one man lighting eight candles and another man singing, and they both have beards. Is it the Jewish Christmas?' he asked.

Rabbi Zalman Lent has a good sense of humour and would have appreciated the contradiction of terms with a chuckle. It was he who had arranged the public celebration of Chanukah, the Festival of Lights, in December 2004 and again in 2006.

This festival commemorates the rededication in 165 BC of the Holy Temple in Jerusalem by Judas Maccabeus, the legendary Jewish leader who defeated the Greek enemies after they had destroyed the Temple and exiled the Jews from their land. There was only enough consecrated oil for one day, but miraculously it burned for eight days. To celebrate this miracle, each year in every Jewish home, candles are lit for eight nights. Starting with just one candle, an extra one is added every night.

After the kindling of lights on the large eight-branched Chanukah candelabra, the Lord Mayor of Dublin, Alderman Michael Conaghan, invited the crowd of 150 into the Oak Room, where a kosher reception had been prepared in the spirit of this joyous festival.

This young English-born Rabbi represents the Chabad-Lubavitch movement, a Chassidic group founded 250 years ago, now with 3,000 outreach centres ministering to Jews in the four corners of the earth. Rabbi Lent's particular remit for the Dublin Jewish community is working with the youth, from children and teenagers to students, young professionals and young marrieds. His partner in this work is his wife Rifky—who helps when the young Lents permit it! The rabbi also works with students from abroad and has established a 'Hillel House' type accommodation for them in Dublin, also a place where Irish Jewish students can socialise with Jewish people their own age.

The Lents keep an open house for these young people as well as for community members and visitors from abroad. Their table is never empty—a feature very common in all Lubavitcher homes.

For Jewish festivals, celebrations are arranged which the children attend with great gusto. If the parents are well-behaved, they are also allowed to participate. A greatly appreciated aspect of Rabbi Lent's labours is his *L'Chaim Ireland*, a periodical newsletter for the community appearing at festival times. Apart from many communal announcements, it contains stories and photographs of past happenings and upcoming events in the community, and varied articles of Jewish interest from around the globe.

Public Chanukah candle lighting outside the Mansion House Dublin, 2006, hosted by the Lord Mayor

Chanukah lighting (left–right) Rabbi Zalman Lent, Chief Rabbi Yaakov Pearlman, Lord Mayor Vincent Jackson, Cantor Alwyn Shulman

'Bat Chayil', religious celebration for 12-year-old girls, in the Orthodox synagogue, 1978. This event, similar to a 13-year-old boy's bar mitzvah, was first introduced in the 1970s, although earlier bar mitzvah services for girls took place in the Dublin Jewish Progressive Synagogue.

Taoiseach Bertie Ahern opening the 1997 Irish Travel Trade Fair with Gerry Benson, President of the Association, and his daughter Leah

Adrian (Eddie) Cowan qualified both in medicine and dentistry. He taught at the dental school in Dublin, and eventually became Dean of the dental faculty of the Royal College of Surgeons in Ireland.

Young Dubliner Emma Miller (later Sheena) at Hebrew study at the home of Rabbi and Mrs Mirvis, 1980s

Amelia Stein, photographer

CONTEMPORARY

Amelia Stein is well known for her trademark black and white images, widely displayed since the early 1980s. Much of her work has been commissioned by theatre companies, including The Abbey, The Peacock, Druid Theatre Company, Wexford Festival Opera and the Dublin Theatre Festival, and in the UK, the National Theatre and the Royal Shakespeare Company. Her strong black and white portraits of writers, poets, actors and musicians are well known both in Ireland and abroad.

In 2001 her meticulously crafted images taken at the great Palm House in the National Botanic Gardens, Glasnevin, Dublin, prior to its restoration, were exhibited at the Rubicon Gallery. These were followed in 2002 by *Loss and Memory*, the dark and intimate still lives of her late parents' possessions.

Amelia's father Mendel originally ran the Apollo Gymnasium in Mercer Street (later transferred to Maccabi, the Dublin Jewish Sports Club) where the accent was on wrestling and weightlifting.

Mendel Stein's profession was that of optician, and his shop in Harcourt Road, with its memorable eye-shaped window, was for many years a Dublin landmark until redevelopment sadly swept it away.

In 1991 Amelia Stein mounted an outstanding exhibition in Dublin's Gallery of Photography entitled *Solomon's Children*. The theme was the emigration (known in Hebrew as *Aliyah*) to Israel of the ancient community of Jews of Ethiopia. Fifteen years later the sensitivity of Stein's camera lens continues to excite viewers of that work, copies of which have become prized possessions.

Her images of *Jerusalem Theatre* arising from this visit to Israel were shown in an Arts Council tour of Ireland, and in 2004 Amelia became a member of the Royal Hibernian Academy, Ireland.

Solomon's Children: Ethiopian Jewish child refugee with grandmother in Israel. *Photograph © Amelia Stein*

The 1999 wedding of Taryn Enoch and Andrew Barling, the last wedding to take place in the Adelaide Road Synagogue, which was de-consecrated shortly afterwards due to the declining Jewish population. (Curious visitors may note that the façade of the original building has been retained.)

Museum chairman Gerry Tolkin pictured with founding members of the Irish Jewish Museum in 1985 in the former ladies' gallery of the Walworth Road Synagogue, now part of the Irish Jewish Museum.
Back row (left–right): David Lass, Asher Siev (Vice-Chairman), Gerry Tolkin (Chairman), Ramon Eppel, Asher Benson (Archivist).
Front row (left–right): L-R: Marilyn Taylor, Benny Marks, Joan Lynn, Harold Mushatt, Tania Sless

Edmund Ross, photographer. Edmund's studies in medicine were cut short by a family bereavement, and he entered the photography profession. He and his wife Ann run the well-known studio in Dublin's Grafton Street.

Elaine Brown, née Goldwater, gifted musician and piano teacher, and director of the Jewish community's 1986 smash hit, *Joseph and his Amazing Technicolour Dream Coat*. Her husband, engineer Leslie Brown, has put together a register of all Jewish graves in Ireland. Their younger daughter Melanie is a composer, whose work has been broadcast on RTÉ (Irish) radio.

Edmund Ross starring as Joseph in a 1986 amateur production of *Joseph and his Amazing Technicolour Dream Coat*

Cantor Alwyn Shulman with his sons

Cantor Shulman

CONTEMPORARY

In 1991, when South African born Cantor (leader of synagogue prayers) Alwyn Shulman arrived in Dublin with his Israeli wife Nurit, they felt immediately at home in Ireland. Since then Alwyn has been the cantor of the Dublin Hebrew Congregation, Nurit became head of Hebrew studies at Stratford College, and they have reared three handsome sons, the spitting image of both of them.

A cheerful man, Alwyn delights in a Yiddish joke (Yiddish being the lingua franca of 20th-century European Ashkenazi Jews). On his frequent visits to hospitals to visit sick members of the community, their response to his stories sometimes puts them in danger of bursting stitches.

He prepares boys for their bar mitzvah (religious confirmation at the age of thirteen), when they are 'called up' in the synagogue to read a portion of the Torah (Jewish Holy Law) in Hebrew.

In aid of the victims of the Chernobyl Nuclear Disaster Fund he composed and recorded a disc with Stratford College Choir, and to boost sales, he conducted a performance outside the HMV music store in Grafton Street, Dublin, thus helping to raise several thousand euro for the cause.

Dublin Jewish Progressive Synagogue, 1980

The Dublin Jewish Progressive Congregation

1946–PRESENT

Knesset Orach Chayim, known as 'The Progressives', was founded in 1946 by Larry Elyan, Dr Bethel Solomons (see page 23) and others. The new synagogue was built in 1952 alongside the house in Leicester Avenue, and in 1996, the 50th anniversary year of the congregation, the new extension was consecrated.

In 2002 President Mary McAleese and her husband visited the synagogue, and were welcomed by the late Sue Woolfson, then President of the Congregation, Rabbi Dr Charles Middleburgh, who commutes regularly between Dublin and the UK, and members of the congregation. 'She's the nicest President I ever met!' was the considered opinion of one of the younger children present on that historic occasion.

Envoi

JEWISH DUBLIN TODAY

The Bretzel kosher bakery in Lennox Street, which also attracts large numbers of non-Jewish customers who can be seen in lengthy queues patiently waiting to purchase their famous bagels and rye bread

The state of play of Dublin Jewish institutions is: three synagogues—the orthodox Dublin Hebrew Congregation and the *Machzikei Hadass* in Terenure, and the Progressive Synagogue in Rathgar; three cemeteries—the disused graveyard in Ballybough, the Orthodox in Dolphin's Barn and the Progressive at the foot of the Dublin Mountains.

Those praiseworthy Orthodox and Progressive organisations, the *Chevreh Kadishot* (Holy Burial Societies)—unique groups of communal volunteers who, as a *mitzvah* (good deed) arrange burial of the dead and assistance for the bereaved—are still going strong today.

Of the numerous active youth groups of earlier times, only BBYO (the *B'nai Brith* Youth Organisation) and the Union of Jewish Students of Ireland are still flourishing.

The three schools which make up Stratford College, and also Edmondstown Golf Club—both institutions originally conceived as 'Jewish'—now have non-Jewish majorities. The Jewish Home for senior citizens occupies part of the magnificent new Quaker facility at Bloomfield. The baby of the institutions, the Irish Jewish Museum, 21 years old, continues to attract parties from home and abroad of young and old, fascinated by the tale of Irish Jewry.

In Little Jerusalem there is no sign of the bustling activity of the little Clanbrassil Street shops described by Ray Rivlin (see page 1). However, near the South Circular Road, The Bretzel in Lennox Street—although no longer Jewish owned—continues to sell kosher bread and rolls, as does the KCR in Terenure Road West. Customers looking for kosher groceries or the makings of a salt beef sandwich must now travel further south of the Liffey to Supervalu in Churchtown or Tesco in Nutgrove.

In general, not all those who have come to Ireland as asylum-seekers or immigrants from European Union countries have yet identified themselves with the Dublin Jewish community. Perhaps this book may encourage more of them to do so.

Asher Benson
October 2006

Index